Support Services
and
the Curriculum

Support Services
and
the Curriculum

A Practical Guide to Collaboration

Penny Lacey and Jeanette Lomas

David Fulton Publishers
London

David Fulton Publishers Ltd
2 Barbon Close, London WC1N 3JX

First published in Great Britain by
David Fulton Publishers 1993

British Library Cataloguing in Publication Data

A catalogue record for this book is available from the British Library

ISBN 1-85346-222-5

Typeset by Action Typesetting Limited, Gloucester
Printed in Great Britain by The Cromwell Press Limited, Melksham, Wiltshire

Contents

Figures

Foreword

by Ron Davie

This book is timely. Support services for children with special educational needs (SEN) have been under threat since the Education Act 1988. The 1993 Education Act reinforced that trend. Most of the threat derives from the simplistic application of the 'market forces' ideology which underpins much of this legislation.

The threat operates on three levels. At its most general, there is an implicit − sometimes explicit − rejection of local authority based education services. Of course, support services for children with SEN also operate from within schools. Nevertheless, centrally based SEN support services have been caught up in the government's seeming reluctance to see any significant contribution to, or oversight of, schools by local authorities.

The second threat to such support services has again derived from their being caught up in a wider ideological debate. The government has been persuaded that schools have become too 'child-centred' and not concerned enough with the 'three R's'. Part of the blame for this alleged state of affairs has been laid at the door of teacher training establishments but also of local authority advisers and inspectors, who, it is said, are too 'theoretical' in their approach. Whatever the validity of this perspective, it can not sensibly be related to support teams in SEN contexts; and yet the new broom of radical educational reform has a tendency to sweep all before it.

The third strand of the current threat to SEN support services lies in the failure of the recent educational legislation to come to terms with the nature of special education needs. The original 1988 Education Act had clearly paid little regard to the needs of the 20% or so of children whom the 1981 Education Act had addressed. Subsequent moves on this front by the Department of Education and Science (later, Department for Education) and the National Curriculum Council were often therefore in the nature of damage limitation. The White Paper on 'Choice and Diversity' (DFE, 1992) which preceded the 1993 Education Bill – and then the Bill itself, as originally drafted – paid no regard to the need for a range of support services for children with SEN to be maintained at local authority level. Fortunately, wiser counsels prevailed and a government amendment requiring local authorities to maintain such services – albeit within a customer-contractor framework – was inserted into the Bill.

The combined effect of this tripartite threat was often devastating. It struck not only at the professional and structural basis for the existence of SEN support services but at the job security of the individuals involved. Until the above government amendment to the 1993 Education Bill, many SEN support teams had been in the process of breaking up. Indeed, the amendment was too late to save the loss of precious expertise in many areas, as advisory teachers and other transferred to other fields.

The timeliness of this book thus in part relates to the necessary rebuilding of morale and expertise in the often denuded SEN support teams of the early 1990's. Paradoxically, though, this situation may also – at least in part – provide some opportunities for breaking or side-stepping at least some of the 'stumbling blocks' which the authors describe so clearly in Chapter Two.

The problems they set out are in some measure a feature of any process of institutional change. In addition, in this specific context, they have the further dimension of difficulty arising from inter-professional boundaries, rivalries, etc. The combined strength of these two factors in resisting change is formidable, and has a long history (Davie 1993a and 1993b). However, the very turbulence which I have referred to above could in some ways provide contexts which might help break the mould. Thus, as we know, external threats can have the effect of turning a group in upon itself and reducing the possibility of co-operating with others. However, external threats may also impel a group to look for allies. Close reading of Lacey's and Lomas's detailed anatomy of the position would be invaluable in helping to facilitate the latter and inhibit the former.

Introduction

Over the last twenty years, there has been much encouragement of multi-disciplinary teamwork to meet the needs of children with special educational needs. The writers of both The Court Report (DHSS, 1976) and The Warnock Report (DES, 1978) recognised the importance of professionals working together to define and meet the needs of children and both reports contributed considerably to the development of practices subsequently. Despite the interest, genuine teamwork of a multi-disciplinary nature has been very difficult to achieve. It is relatively easy to argue for a unified approach to the needs of children, but quite another for this to happen in practice. Tomlinson wonders whether we are being naive asking for it all. 'The development of extended multi-professional assessments, advocated by both the Court and Warnock Reports ... assumes an unrealistic degree of communication, co-operation and absence of professional conflicts and jealousies' (Tomlinson, 1982, p.31). Although Tomlinson's view is helpful in that it encourages a deeper study of the possible barriers to working across disciplines and specialisms, members of teams need practical guidance on how to overcome these problems. It is not enough to exhort professionals to work together and then leave them to it. Staff need both time and training to make best use of each other's skills and experience.

This book has been conceived with that practical guidance in mind. It is full of suggestions and examples, all of which are based on reality. Our own personal experiences have contributed considerably to the text and these have been placed alongside observations of colleagues at work and results of discussions. We have tried not to make suggestions that could be used to accuse us of living in an 'ivory tower', but we take seriously our need to demonstrate possibilities, however far from your own experience they may seem at the moment.

We have placed support services at the centre of the book but we extend this term to include support staff of any kind. Anyone who contributes to the education and welfare of pupils in mainstream and special schools is included. We have also given a central place to the curriculum and the ways in which support staff can work closely with class and subject teachers to enable all children to have access to a curriculum suitable for them. We have, of course, included parents in our deliberation, although we have not singled them out often for specific discussion. We would just reiterate the importance of *everyone* working together to meet needs.

We will begin with a summary of the main points made in the book as a guide for you, the reader. All the points are taken up and expanded in the text and although reading every section will mean you cover everything, selected reading is certainly possible. Each section is designed to be reasonably self contained.

Why collaborate?

Throughout this book we use the term 'collaboration' and this is defined in Chapter 1. We chose this particular word to describe the way in which professionals should work together as it is relatively jargon-free. One of the biggest barriers to multi-discplinary work is competing jargon and we want to contribute to reducing this problem.

The list that follows sums up the main points supporting the notion of using collaboration to meet the diverse needs of pupils in mainstream and special schools. These are expanded in following chapters.

- There is no one body responsible for children with special educational needs, thus many agencies and individuals are involved and their work needs to be co-ordinated.
- Special needs are so diverse that no one professional could meet them all.
- The needs of the whole child can be met. There is a tendency for each professional only to have an interest in the part of the child for which he or she is responsible (the ears or mobility or language skills etc.).
- The child can experience an integrated response to his or her needs, particularly through a whole curriculum approach.
- Working in partnership with families and carers can better meet the daily living needs of children with special needs.

- If every person involved with the child is working towards the same goals then there can be maximum practice of skills. The emphasis for different specialists may vary, but through discussion priorities can be agreed.
- New needs can be identified immediately by anyone involved with the child. Subsequent specialist advice can be sought if necessary.
- There can be the minimum of unnecessary overlap of e.g: assessment and resources.
- Collaborative problem-solving produces more innovative results than individuals working alone. The synergetic feature of teamwork ensures that 'the whole is greater than the sum of the parts'.
- Professional development can be in-built as members of the team engage in reflection and practical problem-solving together.
- The rights of the child can be better protected if more than one person work together. It is more likely that needs will really be met.

Problems with collaboration

As indicated at the beginning, collaboration is difficult to achieve. Recognising some of the problems encountered goes some way towards trying to solve them. The next list sums up particular problems or 'stumbling blocks' encountered in England. Many have a history in the fact that services have always been divided and competing in nature.

- Education, Health, Social Services and voluntary agencies have separate funding, management, hierarchies, training and philosophies which makes understanding between professionals difficult.
- There are historical professional barriers and vested interests to be overcome. This is particularly evident in the presence of jargon and the tendency for professional stereotyping.
- There can be problems concerning the financial implications for collaborative decisions. Who pays for what?
- Status differentials mean that it is hard for collaborating professionals to feel they can contribute equally. Teams of unequals containing doctors tend to be dominated by them.

- Codes of practice for confidentiality make sharing records difficult.
- Many professionals have very large case loads and are thus members of many different teams. This can lead to divided loyalties.
- If there is no regular contact between services, advice from one can be based on inaccurate information about what another can provide.
- The word 'team' can be a misnomer. Goals and priorities have not been agreed, members hardly ever meet, conflict is feared so discussion is superficial and children receive disjointed individual programmes.
- There is very little joint training in collaborative work and interpersonal skills.
- Professionals who are used to working autonomously feel threatened by working with others. They are also used to working directly with the child in their own specialism and have few skills for sharing.
- Collaborative work tends to take longer, especially at first and this frustrates many people, especially if the quality of team meetings is poor.

These and other difficulties are discussed at various points in the book. Some are addressed in great detail, for example the chapters on working together in teams and joint training for collaboration.

Effective collaboration

The third set of statements sum up the ideal of working together collaboratively. The discussions later expand on the suggestions and demonstrate how they can be achieved.

- Individuals understand each other's training, skills, experience, philosophy and the constraints under which they work.
- There is good utilisation of individual's resources, both personal and those invested through role.
- Role edges are blurred so everyone meets the needs of the whole child but not to the extent that specialisms are obliterated and complementary skills lost.
- There is recognition that not everyone needs to be equal and that leadership of the team will vary according to priorities for the child.

- Conflict is a constructive force, enabling many different views to be presented and discussed. No-one feels threatened, there is a general feeling of support and a desire to learn from each other to meet the needs of individual children.
- There is a commitment from all members to keep up-to-date in their specialisms and maintain an 'action research' attitude to their work.
- Training in collaborative work is recognised as important and this influences the organisational aspects of the team.
- There is shared record-keeping which is truly informative.
- Meetings are well run and decisions are made. There is trust amongst members so that full meetings are not always needed to make decisions.
- There are regular reviews, not only of the progress of the children but of the work of the team. Staff and team training are regarded as important and time is set aside for relevant development.
- It is recognised that a fully fledged team is not always necessary. Sometimes a looser network of professionals offering occasional input to a keyworker or a small inner group is more efficient in terms of time and effort.

Suggestions for making collaboration easier

The final area we would like to present at this time concerns a summary of what we feel could be accomplished with commitment from those involved at various levels. We feel we have little influence at legislative level but can, at least, suggest that many problems would be solved if there was one state department for children and their needs. Realistically this will not come about in the near future. At strategic level, local authority decision makers need to be more aware of and more involved in inter-agency work. The Children Act (1989) is forcing this in the area of child protection. This needs to extend to other aspects of work with children.

Work at operational level includes heads of services and schools and some heads of departments in large schools. At this level there needs to be commitment to facilitating collaboration at fieldworker level, the so-called 'chalk-face'. Managers must recognise the importance of timetabling, organising resources and suitable joint training. The following list contains the main points which will enable this to happen.

- Good relationships between services at strategic level achieved through genuinely open discussions and a commitment to working together to meet the needs of children with special needs.
- Specific individuals appointed to manage inter-agency collaboration at strategic and operational levels.
- Job descriptions at all levels to contain reference to collaboration.
- Written contracts between services to contain specific collaborative elements.
- Agreement across services for 'extended confidentiality' so that team members in the field can share relevant information on individual children.
- Written guidelines for working in partnership with families and carers which is subject to regular review.
- A key worker to be named for every child to co-ordinate the input from the various professionals, call relevant meetings and be responsible for compiling and circulating written reports. Duties should be written into the job description of the key worker and regularly reviewed.
- A shared physical location for team members to ease the problems of communication and professional barriers.
- Clustered case loads for peripatetic staff to cut travelling time and numbers of in-house staff with whom to liaise.
- Active managerial support e.g.: time allowed for meetings/ telephones available for ease of contact/secretarial support for written reports etc.
- Financial support and time allowed for joint training both in aspects of the needs of the children and in effective collaboration.
- Regular review of the effectiveness of inter-agency collaboration at all levels (legislative, strategic, operational and in the field).

Implementing these suggestions would go some way towards responding to the criticisms of HMI (1991) in their report *Interdisciplinary Support for Young Children with Special Educational Needs*. There is much of interest to primary and secondary education in this report, despite the fact that it relates specifically to pre-school children. The main findings include:

> 3. Where less than satisfactory provision occurred it was associated with poor co-ordination of the various services available for the

under-fives, a lack of clear definition in the roles of the workers and an absence of recognised leadership and structures.

6. Where in-service training for professional groups was available it was well supported but there were few opportunities for joint training for members of interdisciplinary teams.

(HMI, 1991, p.1)

The contents of this book are intended to be a starting point. We begin with an overview of support services and the problems and possibilities that exist in their work. We then move to the curriculum and assessment and consider how staff can work together to enable children to receive a unified curriculum best suited to their needs. The next section contains a chapter on how staff can develop effective teamwork and the kinds of training available to help this come about. The final part is entitled 'The Way Forward' and this consists of the structure for conducting an audit and developing an action plan for the future.

There are many examples of current practice given throughout the book which you may find relate to your present situation. You will, no doubt, be able to offer more to illustrate the points covered. We hope that our enthusiasm for collaborative working will be conveyed in the following chapters and that you will find our practical ideas of value as you strive to meet the diverse needs of the pupils in your care.

Part I

Support Services: An Overview

CHAPTER 1

Support Services – Their Growth and Current Practice

What is a support service?

The term 'support' is used to describe various groups of people offering advice and skills to aid the integration, and general education, of children with difficulties in learning. We read of schools having a 'Support Department' with 'support teachers' who offer 'learning support' or 'curriculum support', or 'special needs support'. Non-school based services often use the term 'special needs support team' or 'support service' as in 'peripatetic support service for children who are visually impaired'. However, Hart (1986) states that there is 'no generally agreed definition of support teaching'. Support services and support/advisory teachers are discussed as if there is a nationally agreed definition, whereas in reality support services differ according to their function, role, development, personnel and the Local Education Authority who employs them. The variety of jobs undertaken by learning support teachers can vary from making a Christmas cake with a group of children with language difficulties to running round the track with an educationally blind child. More examples are given by Booth *et al.* (1987).

In 1986 the Journal *Remedial Education* changed its name to *Support for Learning* a transformation which demonstrates a shift in thinking and which gives a more positive view of the role of support staff. The 1980s were the years when LEAs and schools changed their ethos and moved towards meeting the diverse needs of pupils experiencing difficulties in learning. Before the Warnock Report (DES, 1978) and the 1981 Education Act, schools generally held the belief that children with learning difficulties were best helped by being removed from the mainstream curriculum. Teachers who worked with these children were said to teach the 'remedial groups' and were expected to undertake traditional remedial teaching concentrating on improving literacy skills. It was very rare for the 'remedial' teacher to work in the classroom alongside the class teacher. Segregation to integration, withdrawal to in-class support, isolation to collaboration are elements which have slowly been evolving in the 1980s and in this chapter we aim to look at this development. The rapid growth of support services over the last twelve years will be briefly examined along with who constitutes a member of a support team, the type of support offered and some of the terminology used.

The growth of support services

A number of initiatives in the 1970s and early 1980s encouraged considerable changes in the English and Welsh education systems which improved the educational opportunities for children and young people with disabilities. The 1970 Education (Handicapped Children) Act made Local Education Authorities responsible for the education of *all* children, however severely disabled. It stated that all local school systems in England and Wales should provide every child with the opportunity to be educated.

In 1974, The Warnock Committee, chaired by Mary Warnock was established to look at special education. Their brief was very wide and it took them four years to produce their report, *Special Educational Needs* (1978).

The Warnock Report, as it is generally known, has had a considerable effect upon the whole of education. The report stated that approximately 20 per cent of school-age children would have special educational needs during their school years and, as a consequence, may require additional resources. Special needs could arise from sensory impairment, physical disability, learning difficulties, emotional or behavioural problems, or any combination. This book is concerned with the specialist support for all 20 per cent whether in special schools (2 per cent) or in mainstream education (18 per cent).

The type and degree of support that individuals require to meet their special needs will be as diverse and individual as their identified needs. Services visit all schools covering all age and ability ranges. If support is not available then identified pupils will be severely limited in their ability to benefit from a broad, balanced, relevant and differentiated curriculum.

The Warnock Committee stated 'we wholeheartedly support the principle of the development of common provision for all children' (7.3). The chapter which concentrates on special education in the mainstream examined various forms of integration and the ingredients necessary to make them successful. Particular emphasis is given to appropriate specialist training and the need for a high level of support from various services plus the right range of facilities. The report indicated that successful integration could not be achieved 'on the cheap'. This view was supported by Hegarty and Pocklington (1981) who argue that a policy of integration which has the necessary level of support is as costly as the alternatives.

While carrying out their investigations the Committee found that the few existing advisory services for children with special needs were fragmented, with no clear policies or shared perspectives. Warnock called for all special education services to be unified into one, containing:

- advisory teachers who could offer advice to an identified number of mainstream schools;
- specialist teachers who could work directly with the children;
- advisers; and
- senior adviser.

(DES, 1978, 13.20)

Whether such a model exists today is very debatable.

The concept of collaboration between support services in special education arises directly out of the recommendations of the Warnock Committee, the Report states: 'The development of close working relationships between professionals in the different services concerned with children and young people with special needs is central to this report' (DES, 1978, 16.1). Warnock saw the importance of working together to meet the needs of the whole child and family and could see how medical, social services and education personnel would work together for their total good.

Legislation over the past decade has reinforced the need for more collaborative working between professionals, The Warnock Report (1978) culminating in The 1981 Education Act, The 1986 Disabled Persons Act and The Children Act (1989) have wide ranging implications for children with disabilities. Their welfare is of 'paramount' consideration and this requires local authorities to work in partnership with parents, and other agencies to minimise the effect of a disability and provide the opportunity for the children to lead lives which are as 'normal' as possible.

Clarification of terminology

In order for support services to work effectively to ensure a unified, balanced approach to the family and their child with special needs, a collaborative approach must be adopted and is advocated throughout this book. Various terms are used to describe groups of professionals working together, i.e. multi-disciplinary, inter-disciplinary, and transdisciplinary or collaborative. The first two models appear to fall short of the ideal concept of a team approach, which supports the whole child and family, across the whole curriculum, while the latter is the model of support service delivery that provides the structure to enhance collaborative working.

The multi-disciplinary team

This term and approach appears to have grown out of the medical model where experts in various areas bring their particular knowledge to the case of a patient. It is commonly seen at the initial stages of diagnosis and during the formal assessment procedures. The child is examined/assessed by a team from various disciplines all of whom have the common aim of identifying the child's level of functioning and special needs. This model of approach has evolved as there has been a move towards seeing the child as a whole and a realisation that knowledge of the various aspects of the child must be integrated in order that he/she can achieve the maximum from their education.

The degree of importance placed upon the information gained from the contributing professionals often varies according to their character and status and the setting where the advice is given, be it in a medical, educational, social service or home setting.

On many occasions the multi-disciplinary approach results in a child being seen by a number of professionals and then the information being sent to one member of the team or, as in the case of the 1981 Education Act assessment procedure, a statementing officer. Therefore a group decision is not made as to the best procedures to be followed. Those who have been members of a multi-disciplinary team can state that there is a high possibility of conflicting recommendations, and if the person collating reports

Figure 1.1 A Multi-disciplinary Approach

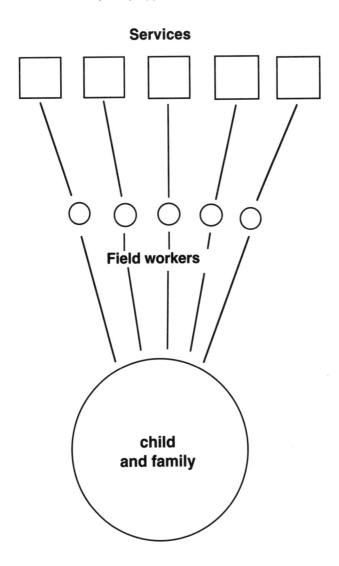

does not have certain knowledge and expertise, the implications of some of the recommendations may be lost and omitted from the final report or 'statement'.

Fig 1.1 — the multi-disciplinary model — demonstrates the way in which the professionals work in isolation without collaborative decisions being achieved regarding the implementation of recommendations, teaching approaches, or resources.

The inter-disciplinary approach

On recognition of some of the limitations of the multi-disciplinary approach, as outlined above, many professionals have adopted an inter-disciplinary approach. The team is made up of the same members as in the multi-disciplinary model but there is an attempt to control the fragmentation of findings. The child is seen by the various team members. This is frequently done individually but a group meeting then takes place so that recommendations can be fully discussed. In this way each member of the team (which should include the parents) contributes to the discussion and decision-making process.

There are many similarities between the multi-disciplinary and the inter-disciplinary approaches. Each rely upon all team members having the necessary skills to carry out their assessment effectively and produce a report containing the appropriate recommendations. The recommendations are usually concerning the type and amount of intervention required. However, in many cases the availability of resources, both human and material, are not always considered and the ideal, instead of the manageable, is presented. While it can be argued that all children should receive the best, it is undoubtedly the class teacher who has the responsibility of implementing the recommendations when he/she often feels the least able, with the least authority and with no resources.

Another weakness of the above two approaches is the lack of follow-up with regard to the recommendations. Many professionals involved in the initial assessment do not have regular contact with the child and may only become involved at a time of crisis. An example may be the educational psychologist who may provide advice for the statement of special educational needs. The recommendations contained in the report may suggest the type of programme required by the child but will not state the amount of support to be given to the class teacher in order to implement the programme. Due to the demands of large caseloads the educational psychologist may not have contact with the child and teacher until some crisis occurs or the child's annual review is due.

Fig 1.2 illustrates how the interdisciplinary model is constructed.

The transdisciplinary or collaborative approach

This approach has been advocated in the USA by Hutchinson (1974) who discussed the advantages by examining the United Cerebral

Figure 1.2   An Inter-disciplinary Approach

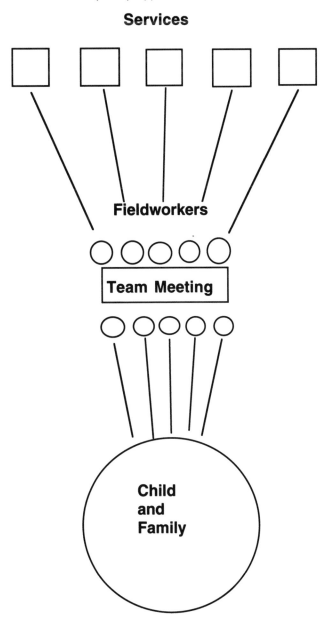

Services

Fieldworkers

Team Meeting

**Child
and
Family**

Palsy Collaborative Infant programme. The approach evolved in an attempt to overcome the problems identified above. In order to reduce the fragmentation and compartmentalising of services, one person is appointed for direct contact for the child and family. The initial assessment is carried out in the same way as the two approaches above and the recommendations may be agreed as in the inter-disciplinary approach, but the implementation of the recommendations is carried out by a few people in co-operation with the others.

The composition of the team for the collaborative approach to supporting children with diverse needs will depend upon the identified special needs of the child and family and may appear the same as the multi-disciplinary and inter-disciplinary models, however, the personal qualities of the individual members of the trans-disciplinary/collaborative team should be such that they can work as a collaborative member of the team, demonstrating a willingness to share expertise, assume some of the responsibilities of the other team members and become a learner in addition to a specialist. (See the chapters on Working in Teams and Training for further discussion.)

We have chosen the term 'collaborative' rather than the American sounding 'transdisciplinary' because we want to present a model which is jargon free, and which clearly describes the method of working. Our collaborative model contains the majority of aspects described in the transdisciplinary approach, however, the major difference is that the identified link/'named' (Warnock)/key person, will change as the child progresses through education and the team will address the needs of the *whole* child across the *whole* curriculum.

Fig 1.3 offers a diagrammatic representation of how the transdisciplinary or collaborative approach can work.

Fig 1.4 (p.20) is taken from Orelove and Sobsey (1991). It compares each model by examining aspects of work covered by a team of professionals working with a child with special needs.

Membership of support teams

The members of a collaborative team will be as varied as the child's special needs. The professionals identified as having contact with the child who has diverse needs are employed by the public sector, from the district health authority, the local education authority, social services – the 'triangle of provision' (Freeman and Gray, 1989) and the voluntary sector. With the growth of input from voluntary agencies we would like to include them in 'service providers' and therefore use the phrase 'Rectangle of provision' (see Fig 1.5).

Figure 1.3   Transdisciplinary or Collaborative Approach

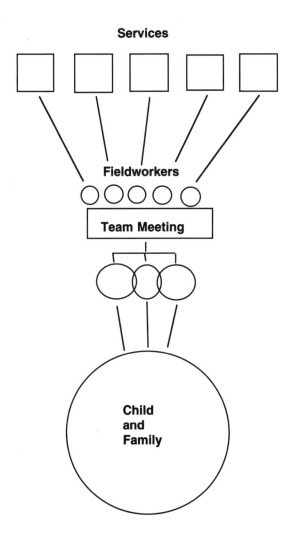

Figure 1.4   A Comparison of the Three Approaches

	Multi-disciplinary	Inter-disciplinary	Transdisciplinary/ collaborative
Assessment	Separate assessments by team members	Separate assessments by team members	Team members and family conduct a comprehensive development assessment together
Parent participation	Parents meet with individual team members	Parents meet with team or team representative	Parents are full, active, and partici-pating members of the team
Service Plan Development	Team members develop separate plans for their discipline	Team members share their separate plans with one another	Team members and the parents develop a service plan based upon family priorities, needs and resources
Service Plan Responsibility	Team members are responsible for implementing their section of the plan	Team members are responsible for sharing information with one another as well as for implementing their section of the plan	Team members are responsible for how the primary service provider implements the plan
Service Plan Implentation	Team members implement the part of the service plan related to their discipline	Team members implement their section of the plan and incorporate other sections where possible	A primary service provider is assigned to implement the plan with the family
Lines of Communication	Informal lines	Periodic case-specific team meetings	Regular team meeting where continuous transfer of information, knowledge and skills are shared among team members
Guiding Philosophy	Team members recognise the importance of contributions from other disciplines	Team members are willing and able to develop, share, and be responsible for providing services that are a part of the total service plan	Team members make a commitment to teach, learn and and work together across discipline boundaries to implement unified service plan
Staff Development	Independent and within their discipline	Independent within as well as outside of their discipline	An integral component of team meetings for learn-ing across disciplines and team building

Source: Orelove and Sobsey (1991)

Figure 1.5   The 'Rectangle' of Service Provision

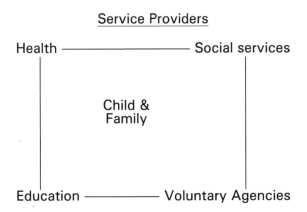

The Association for the Education and Welfare of the Visually Handicapped (AEWVH) and the Royal National Institute for the Blind (RNIB) Joint Working Party for Children who are Multi-handicapped and Visually Impaired (MHVI) examined the number of professionals who come into contact with children who have multiple disabilities in addition to defective sight, and their families. The number, in some cases, was a staggering twenty-seven (see Fig. 1.6, 1992, RNIB Report). Each professional had very different skills and offered differing types of support throughout the child's first nineteen years of life. How the skills were used very much depended upon the systems employed.

Each member of the team will have a different perspective on the child's needs and will have a distinct role to play within the team. The collaborative approach encourages the contribution of all members including the parents who, although not strictly 'professional', in that they have not had any formal training, have very valuable information about their child and consequently must be viewed as essential team members.

Each member of the support team will have certain skills which can aid the child and family. Each will have a different line manager and a different level of involvement. There is an essential need for initial support to be well organised and managed so that there is not a conflict of information and advice given nor a duplication of resources. Warnock (1978) identified the need to co-ordinate services and anticipated the possibility of conflict when so many agencies are involved. This issue will be discussed in the next chapter when we outline some of the 'stumbling blocks' to effective working experienced by support staff.

Figure 1.6   Professionals who may be involved with Children with MHVI and their Families

Class teacher
Non-teaching assistant
Geneticist
Physiotherapist
IT specialist
Speech therapist
Optometrist
Paediatrician
Mobility instructor
Orthoptist
Music therapist
Technical officer for the VI
Educational psychologist
Service for the hearing impaired
Peripatetic teacher of VI
Consultant ophthalmologist
Educational audiologist
Orthopaedic surgeon
General practitioner
Dentist/dental surgeon
Residential social worker
Barnardo fostering team
Clinical psychologist
Community mental handicap team
Occupational therapist
Paediatric neurologist
Portage worker
Massage therapist
Dietician
Chiropodist
Aromatherapist

Parents

'Parents as partners' is a phrase constantly used within education, however, whether this view is held by all who may be members of a collaborative team is under question. This concept, which was clearly defined in The Plowden Report (1967), became popular after the Warnock Report and has recently been strengthened by The Children Act 1989 and The Parents' Charter (1991a). The 1981 Act (implementing some of the recommendations of the Warnock Report) expanded and improved the old style Special Education forms, which recorded children in different categories of disability, making them accessible to parents and emphasised the need for parents to be involved in all stages of their child's assessment and statementing procedures.

Screening and statementing procedures

Collaborative working starts at the time when all infants are screened by primary health teams. Screening is a medical term and is a search for infants experiencing health problems in their early years. Within the first ten days there will be close examination of the child to note:

- any illness
- any defects
- weight
- length
- circumference of the head.

(Lindsay, 1984, p.23)

After this babies will be seen regularly by a doctor or health visitor. In Sheffield developmental and physical assessments are carried out at:

- 6 weeks
- 6 months
- 1 year
- 2 years
- 3 years
- 4 years and
- a school entry medical examination near the child's fifth birthday.

These regular assessments are not always possible (Powell in Lindsay, 1984) and increasingly we are seeing children screened by their general practitioner's 'well-baby' clinics.

The majority of health authorities assess according to Sheridan's four fields of development:

- Posture and body movement
- Vision and fine movement
- Hearing and language: expressive and comprehension
- Play and social behaviour.

(Sheridan, 1975)

The identification and assessment of pupils having special needs is undertaken by professionals from health, social services, education and, increasingly, the voluntary sector. This may be when a child is only a few months old or it may not be until the child has started formal education. The 1981 Act stated that, wherever possible, a child's needs should be met within the mainstream and if a Statement of Special Educational Needs, according to Section 5 of the Education Act 1981 is deemed necessary, it should consist of advice from a multi-disciplinary team. According to Circular 22/89, paragraph 29, 'these procedures focus upon a group of children within the larger group of children with special educational needs' (DES, 1989a).

Statements can be written for children from as young as a few months of age to nineteen years. The process involves gathering advice from an educational psychologist, a doctor, the parents and other relevant professionals such as speech therapists, physiotherapists, social worker or teacher. The advice is sent to the statementing officer who, according to the Audit Commission (1992) should reach a decision within six months concerning the issuing of a statement. If a Statement of Special Educational Needs is deemed necessary then it will consist of five sections:

(i)   Introduction, which gives bibliographical information about the child and parent/guardian.

(ii)   Special educational needs of the child as assessed by the education authority.

(iii)   Special educational provision,
a) which the education authority consider appropriate to meet the needs specified in Part ii,
b) any modifications to the National Curriculum – in terms of programmes of study, attainment targets and assessment and testing,
c) any exemptions from foundation subjects and
d) details of how the exempted programmes will be replaced to maintain a broad, balanced curriculum.

(iv)   Appropriate school or other arrangements and

(v)   Additional non-educational provision.

In their research, Goacher et al. (1988) came to the conclusion that many statements were concerned mainly with the relocation of children and that the provision was decided before the needs were fully examined.

Collaboration of services, however, should not only exist for the 2 per cent of children who are the subject of a Statement of Special

Educational Needs, but there should also be collaboration to ensure that the difficulties experienced by all pupils are addressed in an agreed format. In an ideal world statements would only be necessary where there is a dispute over existing resources and not as the only means of getting additional support. Mainstream schools should be encouraged to cater for a diversity of pupils and there should be a continuum of provision.

Type of support given

Visiting support services

Many support staff have adapted their form of service delivery and now offer three different forms:

- direct;
- indirect; and
- a combination of the two.

Direct support is that which is given to the child by the support member of staff, be that a specialist teacher, classroom assistant or a therapist. Indirect support is the specialist giving advice and information to the class teacher. This advice then directly affects the child's programme. The support staff act as 'consultants', sharing their knowledge and expertise with the teacher and working indirectly through them. The following scenarios illustrate the difference between the three models.

1. Susan is taken by John Smith, the specialist teacher for the visually impaired into the staffroom where work is undertaken to develop visual search and scan skills. He works for half an hour using 2D materials which he has brought in from his base at a special school for children with impaired vision. After the session Susan rejoins her class and the specialist teacher tells the class teacher that Susan requires more practice at visually searching and scanning 2D pictures.

2. John Smith, the specialist teacher, of the visually impaired, meets with Ann Lee – Susan's class teacher to ask about Susan's progress. Ann states that Susan appears to be having difficulty with some of the books being used for project work. The class teacher also finds that Susan is easily distracted and does not finish the work she is given. John asks for details about the books used, Susan's position in class and the

teaching approach used for the topic work. As Ann gives the information John is able to suggest possible alternative strategies. The discussion points are then summarised. John leaves to go to another school and Ann goes into class to put into practice the ideas gathered. John Smith writes a summary and sends a copy to Ann.

3. John Smith, the specialist teacher of the visually impaired, meets with Ann Lee – Susan's class teacher, during the morning break in order to discuss the work he intends to carry out with Susan after playtime. John shows Ann the equipment he has brought into school and the record sheet he will use to note responses. Ann explains the work that her mainstream reception children are undertaking, centred around the theme of 'Change'. John asks to borrow the story book 'A very Hungry Caterpillar'. He works with Susan in the classroom thus enabling Ann to see the techniques used to encourage Susan to move her head as she is visually scanning for each item that the caterpillar eats. After the session John discusses his findings and together they think of other activities to develop Susan's visual perceptual skills. They examine the record sheet and agree to keep notes of activities. By the end of the week, John sends a report summarising the aim of the daily search and scan activities, along with suggested materials, the way in which the activities could be extended and presentation guidelines.

In the first scenario Susan has received direct teaching from the specialist teacher whom she sees once every two weeks. This can be identified as part of the 'multi-disciplinary approach' defined earlier. The child is being given direct support as identified on the Statement of Special Educational Needs.

The second, and very contrasting scenario, gives the example of how Susan is supported through an indirect approach. In this approach the specialist teacher acts as a consultant and the teacher is the facilitator. John Smith is able to gather information from the class teacher and offers ideas which the teacher can implement or adapt according to her classroom situation. There is no doubt that the teacher is the key person and Susan is ultimately her responsibility.

In the third example of support a combination of direct and indirect support is offered. Although the specialist teacher is not working directly with Susan on a daily basis he has designed the programme of intervention and has consulted with the teacher so that the activities link in with the work of the rest of the class. He has worked in the classroom with Susan and has gained some indication of the noise and lighting levels, classroom management and Susan's level of concentration when surrounded by her peers. The class teacher has observed the way in which John presented the activities, understands the criteria for assessing the suitability of materials and the need to encourage Susan to use her residual vision. The record sheet becomes clear when explained and consequently Ms Lee feels a valued part of the team. In this example the specialist's professional identity has also been enhanced as he is considered someone who is willing to share knowledge and work within the classroom setting.

In-house support services

In an examination of the type of in-house support available at the beginning of the 1980s, the work by Clunies-Ross and Wimhurst (1983) offers some useful information. In their study of a selection of secondary schools in England and Wales they found that the majority of schools used a combination of classes for 'slow learners', especially for specific subjects, and withdrawal for individual or small group work. There was little evidence of in-class support being available. The survey by Gipps *et al.* (1987) carried out in 1983 demonstrates that there was some movement towards working with individual pupils with difficulties in learning in mainstream classrooms alongside their peers.

In 1978 the Scottish Education Department published a report in which HMIs stated that they believed that pupils with learning difficulties in primary and secondary schools in Scotland were being taught in the wrong way. They believed that to focus attention on remedial education was the wrong approach and called for appropriate education through the whole curriculum. Many of the changes in learning support during the last ten years have stemmed from the aim to widen the curriculum presentation and to offer differentiation to meet the diverse needs of pupils. The National Curriculum Council (1989) stated that 'within any group of pupils there will be a wide range of ability and experience. This calls for a flexible approach allowing for differentiation to provide success and challenges for them all.' Much has been written about differentiation (Weston, 1992; Hart, 1992), but the roots of the term can be found in the

Warnock Report (1978) 'The purpose of education for all children is the same; the goals are the same. But the help that individual children need in progressing towards them will be different.'

Withdrawal

There are many arguments against the system of withdrawal which was so common in the 1970s, not only with regard to the self esteem of the children involved (Woods, 1980), but also the class teachers who could easily feel deskilled and undervalued (Lunt, 1987). When children who experience difficulties in learning are taken out of the classroom setting then it implies that only the 'specialist' teacher has the skills required to provide access to the curriculum thus taking away the responsibility, or ownership by the class teacher (see scenario 1). Collaboration and the exchange of ideas is prevented by such practice.

The 'remedial' services in many schools were fragmented and lacked a clear policy, however, along with the change towards in-class support has been the growth of co-ordinated provision with clear whole school policies.

Through reading the work of Richmond and Smith (1990) and through informal discussions with class teachers, withdrawal work with groups of children experiencing difficulties in the primary setting seems to be a popular form of support. Many teachers argue that joint planning of the programme to be carried out during the withdrawal session can be an effective method for meeting the diverse needs of the pupils. Carefully planned withdrawal which varies according to the task and involves different pupils is not regarded as harmful to the status of the pupils involved or to the perceived skills of the class teacher. The major ingredient required to enable this planning is *time*.

In-class support

In-class support is seen as an effective method of helping pupils who are found to be experiencing difficulties in mainstream lessons. The aims of in-class support are to:

- provide curriculum access to all pupils;
- to examine ways of adapting the curriculum;
- to meet individual needs;
- to ensure that class teachers recognise their responsibilities towards such children; and

● to avoid the stigma which is often associated with withdrawal.

There are many factors which affect the effectiveness of in-class support and the reader is directed to the next chapter for further discussion of some of the 'stumbling blocks' involved. The major factor which must be considered is whether in-class support is considered as support or intrusion. This question is fully debated by Thomas who makes eight recommendations:

1. the whole school community should be involved in developing a policy on classroom team membership;
2. tensions created by the mismatch between concerns and expectations of team members should be avoided;
3. clear task and role definitions should exist to prevent stressful situations;
4. planning for teaming should be undertaken by all participants;
5. individuals' strengths and weaknesses should be identified during the planning stage;
6. clear definition of classroom tasks and activities should be made during planning;
7. the composition of the team needs to be considered carefully;
8. the team needs to meet regularly to discuss and evaluate the way that they have been working.

(Thomas, 1992, p.204)

There must be close examination of the support offered and strategies must be in place to avoid the stresses and tensions common in many classroom teams.

While the majority of teachers involved in in-class support would recognise the need for joint planning, the shortage of planning time is always identified as a problem for this practice. The need for agreement about the aims of the support, how it should be provided, the way the classroom is managed and the style of discipline is covered by Garnett (1988). She lists eight questions to consider before the class teacher and the support member of staff start working together.

1. What can the two teachers (professionals) do to establish a harmonious working relationship before they start working together in the classroom?
2. How can the two teachers find time to liaise?
3. How often do they need to meet outside the classroom?
4. In what ways can the support teacher help with planning and preparation?

5. What resources do they need and which of them is going to prepare what?
6. Should they work out a joint record system?
7. How will they evaluate the effectiveness of their joint work?
8. How can classroom order and discipline be managed when the support teacher is present?

(Garnett, 1988, p.96)

The credibility of the support teacher can rest upon these questions being answered and an agreement concerning such factors being in place before the two members of staff enter the classroom together.

The status of support staff who work in-class is frequently confused by pupils and mainstream staff. For this reason many specialist teachers seize the opportunity of teaching mainstream classes for part of the week. Visiting support staff can prove that they are capable of class teaching by offering to take the lead during a lesson thus freeing the class teacher to work with the children with difficulties in learning.

Joint teaching offered through the system of in-class support should be seen as supporting the whole curriculum, not just providing an alternative approach to covering basic skills in literacy (Richmond and Smith, 1990) or rescuing a poor, uninteresting lesson (Thomas, 1992). The sum of two professionals working together should be greater than one class teacher plus a support member of staff. The effects of two professionals within a classroom should be seen across the whole curriculum.

Current discussion with regard to in-class support in secondary schools is centred around whether this should come from subject specialists or special needs specialists. As one teacher stated 'the experiences I felt supporting in a subject which I had not studied to examination level gave me some understanding of how the child with learning difficulties would feel'. In this way the skills of both teachers can be combined to provide differentiated materials and approaches to the curriculum. This view, however, can be balanced by the fact that it is very difficult to explain a concept or make the relevant adaptations to materials if the support member of staff does not have in-depth knowledge of the subject matter.

Combination of support

As can be seen from scenario 3, in-class support and withdrawal methods of support are not mutually exclusive and much current practice consists of a combination of the two approaches in the overall learning support strategy. This combination of support is considered to be the most effective approach because:

- the class teacher remains the key person and continues to have a major influence on the children's programme;
- there are joint discussions about the teaching approaches and strategies to use with the children, thus giving joint ownership of the ideas developed;
- the class teacher does not feel deskilled;
- the support members of staff gain credibility by demonstrating that they can work 'hands on' in addition to offering advice;
- the children are seen as members of the class and do not appear 'different' and/or 'special';
- the support member of staff can observe the classroom management and organisation style of the teacher and make recommendations which complement the method of working;
- both professionals enhance their skills by learning together.

Influence across the whole curriculum

Warnock's concept of 20 per cent of children experiencing learning difficulties at sometime during their school life has resulted in support services becoming agents of change. Only 2 per cent of children with special needs will be given the protection of a statement, therefore *all* teachers will be teachers of children with diverse needs. Support services can influence the special needs policy of the school, the curriculum and the ways in which staff can differentiate to meet the identified needs of the children. Kelly (1991) describes the aim of support staff as one of initiating change with three aspects – curriculum, attitudes and skills. Whether a permanent member of staff at a school or a visiting specialist, the need to influence curriculum development to meet the diverse needs of *all* children is becoming more apparent. The factors involved in bringing about change and the skills required to implement a whole school policy are not always found to be characteristics of support staff. Reeves (1991) discusses the issues that arose in a secondary school when change was implemented. She calls for explicit training in the change agency role along with the opportunity to work collaboratively with other advisory staff (p.32). Traditionally specialist training has not contained aspects of negotiating, influencing or designing policy documents and as a consequence stress has been caused when such responsibilities as implementing change have been added to the support teacher's role (see Chapter 7 for further discussion).

The impact of the National Curriculum

The 1988 Education Reform Act set down in law a duty on all schools, whether maintained or grant maintained, to provide a common curriculum for all pupils of compulsory school age. This applies to children with learning difficulties whether or not they have a Statement of Special Educational Needs. As there is a legal requirement that all children should have a broad and balanced curriculum, mainstream and support service staff have been encouraged to work together to differentiate the work presented. Support staff have attended in-service courses alongside their mainstream colleagues to decide upon the most appropriate ways to implement the curriculum. Such joint training has had a positive effect upon developing collaboration. For more in-depth discussion about the ways of working together within the whole curriculum see Chapter 4.

Support services are currently feeling threatened by the legislation which has brought about Local Management of Schools and delegated budgets. The growth in the 1980s of provision for children with diverse needs now appears to have been a 'golden age'. Members of support services must look at the work they are providing and ensure that this support is not devalued. Collaborative working to support the whole child in their attempt to gain access to the whole curriculum must not be underrated. Fish (1985) states that one of the handicapping effects on an individual with a disability may be intervention variable:

> Early counselling, and support for families, intervention programmes and supporting services of all kinds from birth to adult life will all be significant. The more effective the inputs, the less handicapping effects.
> (Fish, 1985, p.85)

The effective input described by Fish is increasingly more difficult to achieve. There are many factors which prevent support services providing the level and type of support they feel is necessary. In the next chapter there will be an examination of some of the factors which are frequently cited as 'stumbling blocks' to effective service delivery.

CHAPTER 2

Stumbling Blocks

It has been demonstrated that services offering specialist support for children who have a visual impairment vary considerably from LEA to LEA (Dawkins, 1991). The discrepancy between the quality and frequency is reflected across all areas of special need (Pearson and Lindsay, 1987). The support received by children who are experiencing difficulties, and their teachers, will differ in standard and amount according to the identified need, the part of the country in which they live, and the special needs policy of the education authority and school. In this chapter there will be discussion of some of the difficulties encountered by staff in providing adequate and effective support. The difficulties listed below will also vary in occurrence and degree. We are not suggesting that every service experiences *all* the 'stumbling blocks' which we describe, we are, however, recording common characteristics which have been cited as impairing effective and efficient service delivery.

Management training

Effective support service organisation and delivery can be achieved in various ways with heads of service demonstrating vastly different methods of management to achieve this. Although short courses in educational management are available at various levels, from basic awareness to diploma and degree level, there is little on offer for those who find themselves as the head of a team of teachers who are nomadically covering a wide geographical area trying desperately to offer specialist support. Nor is there management training for those working in schools as special educational needs co-ordinators who are increasingly expected to influence school policies and manage various members of staff.

In the school setting deputy heads, and 'C' allowance post holders in some primary schools, are given the opportunity to develop the many skills required in the management role. The methods used to develop these skills are numerous. They are each given areas of responsibility which are overseen by the head. Deputies and senior management post holders can also learn by 'sitting with Nellie', that is, working alongside the head. Many may state that this can prove to be invaluable in that it can demonstrate ways in which not to carry out a management task in addition to offering examples of good practice. Traditionally courses have been available within LEAs for senior management team members to meet with other similar post holders to:

- explore various approaches to management;
- develop a school policy for an identified area, or
- organise a school budget.

While support staff have not been excluded from applying for such courses these have not been viewed as totally relevant and, in conjunction with limited in-service budgets, more appropriate courses have been sought. Within some LEAs various support services have joined together to target their training needs. However, with the implementation of Education Reform Act (1988), their training has recently been aimed at meeting the changing demands of the National Curriculum and Standard Assessment Tasks, in addition to keeping abreast of developments within their own specialism.

As a consequence, management courses have not been readily available to support service heads who may find themselves with staff to manage, policy documents to write and a budget to control without feeling that they have the necessary skills. In the fields of visual impairment and hearing impairment several heads of services find themselves in the role by default.

Example
Mrs Jones went on a specialist one year training course to gain the qualification of Teacher of the Visually Impaired. Upon returning to her Local Education Authority she presented a paper which outlined the need for a specialist support service. She was given three afternoons per week to identify the need and explore the way forward and this was sufficient to justify the setting up of a service and the recruitment of more staff. Without any management training the role of head of service

was created as the team grew. Although she attended short management courses and completed an Open University 'Managing Schools' course, there was nothing which offered advice specifically to support her as a service head.

Horses for courses

There are several heads of services who, finding themselves in the leading role through the same type of unplanned service growth as outlined above, discover that they do not feel suited to the role and, if they were in a school setting, would not be applying for head teacher posts.

Examples
A. One excellent teacher, who experienced the rapid growth of the service she had initiated, informed her local authority upon the decision to expand the team, that she no longer wanted to lead the service. She felt that someone with management experience should be the next appointment. In her role as deputy head of service she proved to be supportive and knowledgeable about many issues, her confidence grew and it was clear that, although she had leadership qualities and good interpersonal skills she did not possess the management skills and qualities to develop and negotiate the implementation of relevant policies.

B. A young enthusiastic deputy head in a special school in the north-east was successful when he applied for the headship of a school of comparable size in the Midlands. He was delighted when, during the interview, it was revealed that in the near future the school would be moved to a new building. Unfortunately, due to the financial situation of the local authority, the building programme was revised. The education committee decided that the special school should close and resource bases developed along with a substantial growth in the peripatetic service. Without having had experience of the peripatetic role the head of the school found himself, almost overnight, the head of a specialist support service in a large county. It is to his credit that he has made an outstanding head of service.

General difficulties

Ideally, support for pupils with difficulties in learning should be addressed by a collaborative team. The team, having defined common goals, identifies a plan of action to which each member has a complementary part to play. However, this is not easy to achieve as there are some common barriers, or 'stumbling blocks', which prevent effective service delivery.

It is interesting to note the problems listed by Whitaker (1990), with regard to the employment of LEA Advisory Teachers and Inspectors, as several of these have also been frequently stated as difficulties experienced by specialist support staff:

- confusion about rate and allowances for the job;
- non-existent or inadequate job descriptions;
- confusion about terms and conditions;
- lack of clear line management structures;
- lack of information about LEA developments.

Confusion about rate and allowances for the job

Example

In 1991 an LEA decided to review its special needs support services. There was much discussion about the salaries of the various posts. All the five members of the Learning Support Team were receiving 'D' allowances, the head of the peripatetic service for the visually impaired was also on a 'D', while the head of the hearing impaired service was earning a Head Group 2 salary. The remaining members of the services were paid at the main scale plus 'B' allowance. Some support staff were on essential car users allowance and others were not. The lack of clear policy when these services were created became very apparent during the review. As all the above information became public knowledge staff felt increasingly uneasy about their rate of pay. Questions were asked concerning the skills and additional responsibilities of those earning the higher allowances. The confusion soon created dissatisfaction, and the dissatisfaction had an influence upon the quality of service provided.

Non-existent or inadequate job descriptions

Those support services which were created in the late 1970s and early 1980s either have job descriptions which were written as the post developed or have documents which do not truly reflect the work undertaken at the present time (HMI, 1989). Job descriptions in support services have tended to lag behind those within schools and have not changed as rapidly as needs have changed. A clear job description adds to job security and confidence, whereas one which is vague can easily be misinterpreted. The annual review of job descriptions − linked with appraisal − is felt to be the way forward to prevent this 'stumbling block'.

Confusion about terms and conditions

Many support service staff, as in the majority of cases of advisory teachers, are not clear about the terms of their contract. Involvement with parents and other professionals frequently takes place after school or during school holidays. Are support staff then entitled to time off in lieu? The hours and days worked as stated in the Teachers' Pay and Conditions document (1987) do not specify those of support services.

Conway (1989) describes how his LEA developed a number of support services during the 1970s as a response to identified needs and due to specific pressures. 'As a consequence teachers were appointed with different conditions of service, salary structures and management systems' (p.54).

The support staff who are employed by Health or Social Services are frequently unsure about their terms and conditions. They visit children during holidays because they are not governed by school holidays. The difference in holidays has been cited as a 'stumbling block' to effective team work by teachers who have expected visits from such professionals in term time only to discover that they are on annual leave.

Lack of clear line management structures

Some support services do not have a head of service and many support staff in schools do not have a representative on the senior management team. Several of those services that do are unsure about the line manager structure. In certain circumstances they have to refer to an Assistant Education Officer (AEO) for Special Education, in other instances their contact is the AEO for Primary or Secondary, while some support services do not have any AEOs to whom they can refer. Conway (1989), describing the situation in his own LEA recalls that 'at different times the head of service has been responsible to the Principal Educational Psychologists, Senior Assistant Education Officer (Primary and Special Education), the Adviser and the Assistant Education Officer (Special Educational Needs)' (p.54). The headteacher of the school, if the service is school-based, can also be added to this list. Confusion about who is the line manager with regard to policies and the service developments can be a source of stress for heads of service.

This confusion can be equally stressful to those professionals from other disciplines who work regularly with children in the school setting. Their ultimate line manager may be in Health or Social Services, but day to day work may be under the management of the head of a school and as such all support staff should be left in no doubt as to the policies and procedures which should be followed when working in that setting.

Lack of information about Local Authority developments

Davies and Davies (1989) point out that discrepancies frequently exist between support services within LEAs, and that the status of certain support services will depend upon the information which is given. Davies and Davies emphasise the need for support staff to be given support themselves and for Local Education Authorities to 'make evident and explicit their policies and procedures', and that there should be 'clarity and direction for both support services and the recipients of that support' (p.35).

Support services can frequently be overlooked when circulars about developments within a Local Authority are sent out to schools and Health Authority Child Development Centres. Booth *et al.* (1992) state that many National Curriculum Council (NCC) and Schools Examination and Assessment Council (SEAC) documents were not sent to support services in the initial stages of National Curriculum development. The reason given for this oversight being that only schools with DES numbers received all the documentation.

Depending on the profile of a service the head may be invited to policy making meetings, may get minutes from meetings or may read about developments in the local newspaper. For two terms one support service did not receive the usual LEA correspondence while another received two sets! Despite numerous phone calls from each head the discrepancy took six months to rectify.

Professional mystique and vested interests

There is no doubt that when professionals work collaboratively the outcome can be very effective and rewarding for all concerned. However, as Hockley indicates: 'competition sometimes replaces co-operation. Specialisation can fix territorial boundaries, and make attempts towards sharing of responsibility for all pupils very difficult' (1989, p.126).

Where class teachers have been autonomous for many years it takes skilful management and sensitive negotiating skills on the part of the head or senior management team and staff for the support to be collaborative. A whole school approach to meeting special needs is required where the children are seen as the responsibility of the whole school (Hanko, 1989), not just the 'specialists' who either make up the school special needs team or the advisory, peripatetic teacher. Such collective ownership is not achieved overnight and requires careful planning and discussion with all staff members. Hurriedly introduced policies, or those 'imposed from on high' can be a recipe for disaster (Visser, 1986).

Specialist qualifications require additional training and it has been noted that several teachers, once they have undertaken such training, are reluctant to share their skills. They may visit the school, armed with specialist equipment, and neglect to inform the class teacher about the tasks they are doing with the child or what skills the equipment is meant to enhance (see scenario 1, Chapter 1). The mystique surrounding their training can frequently cause a barrier, and the sharing of knowledge can be regarded as devaluing their specialist expertise. It has been stated that by passing on skills 'I will be doing myself out of a job. If I give them all the information and the skills to cope then, under Local Management of Schools, I may be out of a job.'

Using jargon or specialist terminology can cause confusion and stress to others and does nothing to enhance credibility.

Example
At the Case Conference concerning their son Paul, Mr and Mrs Johnson were totally confused by the medical jargon which

was used. The physiotherapist talked about Paul being 'frequently supine, and of his dislike of being prone', she also said he had 'the ATNR', the paediatrician reported that Paul had been 'registered PS on the BD8 form', and the audiologist spoke of a 'conductive hearing loss of 50 dB in both ears'. Even the social worker's report caused some confusion as he spoke of the 'family dynamics' and the 'need for regular respite because the extended family lived over 90 miles away'. All the information given at the Case Conference was shared with Mr and Mrs Johnson after the meeting. In lay person's terms they were told that Paul usually lay on his back because his disliked lying on his stomach, that he had a reflex which meant that when lying on his back with his head turned to the right his right arm would be outstretched with the left arm curled up; that Paul had been registered partially sighted because of his visual loss and that he had a hearing loss due to a problem of the outer ear which could be helped by hearing aids. The social worker wanted to find a suitable family for Paul to stay with every fourth weekend in order to give Mr and Mrs Johnson some time for their other children. This was because their family did not live in the area. The terms used in the case conference were those used within the respective specialism and were not fully understood by those outside that specialism.

Training to encourage support services to share their 'expertise' does not appear to feature within specialist courses. Nor does working with other professionals form a significant part of initial teacher training or Post Graduate Certificate of Education courses. Staff with specialist qualifications should not be viewed as 'experts' as this may cause barriers from the initial visit. It is wiser to view them as colleagues who have had additional or complementary training which can enhance the skills of the class teacher.

If support staff are viewed as 'experts' then they may be viewed as having specialist skills which can solve the intractable problems of others. The 'expert myth' can lead to class teachers disowning problems and expecting instant solutions (Dessent, 1985). When the instant or magic solutions are not forthcoming then a barrier between the class and support member of staff can be created.

Confidentiality

For many years class teachers have felt at a distinct disadvantage when teaching children with diverse needs. This feeling has been fuelled by lack of access to relevant information. Medical records have not been available for teachers to read and much of the information received about children has been 'second or third hand'.

Communicating openly with respect and a sense of professionalism is vital for establishing and sustaining credibility. Information which is given in confidence should not be shared with others. Once confidentiality is broken professionalism will be questioned by all. If a person has had a negative experience with a member of a support team then *all* support staff will be regarded with suspicion. Credibility can be gained through positive experiences. Word of mouth is the way in which services can be made or broken.

Team unawareness and isolation

Some support staff do not view themselves as being a member of a team. They prefer to work on their own without reference to the other members of the team. Many teachers and professionals from other disciplines are reluctant to be a member of a team. They question the need to keep their colleagues informed of their actions. Consequently it is not uncommon to discover that 'wheels' have been reinvented, resources duplicated and conflicting information given. Professional modesty and lack of confidence can be regarded as a contributory factor (Bailey, 1981), but the reluctance to share information should also be viewed as an unawareness of being a team member.

Many support services assume that another adult in a classroom can automatically benefit the pupil with learning difficulties but there is little consideration about whether either teacher has the characteristics to be a team member. The fact that support staff are ill prepared to co-operate and interact with other professionals can cause feelings of isolation. The very nature and size of caseloads given to many specialist teachers can hinder the possibility of them ever having the time within one school to feel part of the team. The class teacher and support staff do not get together to plan or teach and do not follow up activities to the degree where they can 'gel' together and be viewed as a team.

Developing credibility

Developing credibility is vital for all support staff. Davies and Davies (1988) when discussing credibility list the following.

- Developing credibility is achieved by:
  - a sense of professionalism
  - practical skills
  - open communication
  - respect for others
- Legitimate credibility
  - titles and job descriptions initially, supported by a positive experience of effective service delivery
- Reward credibility
  - being able to observe the continuous influence on colleagues' practice
- Referent credibility
  - an awareness of the differing methods, approaches and philosophies within each school
  - a style which respects, acknowledges and responds to these
- Expert credibility
  - a catalyst for ideas and approaches
  - acknowledging the skills already possessed by the class teacher
- Establishing and developing credibility
  Factors to consider:
  - consultation
  - positive professional exchange
  - responsive and flexible approaches
  - perspective and humour
  - parental dialogue.

(Davies and Davies, 1988, pp.13–15)

In order to gain credibility it is essential that the support team member is seen as having the necessary skills and knowledge, or is in a position to gain the information required by the school and parents. We are reluctant to use the term 'expert' because it is felt that children are such individuals that one is always in the learning situation. If support is to be maximised then the information held by the support member of staff must be shared with all relevant personnel and the game of 'knowledge is power' or the 'know it all syndrome' (Bowers, 1984) can be avoided.

Example
Steven Simpson, an educational psychologist working in a
small metropolitan education authority visited Roseberry
School to assess Jane Walker's learning difficulties. He spoke
with her class teacher and asked for copies of records and
reports. Afterwards he worked with Jane in the staff room. At
the end of the morning session Steven left the school without
reporting back to the class teacher. Two weeks later the school
received a report which, according to the class teacher, did not
offer any new information. Steven's credibility was certainly
not enhanced by this lack of communication or acknowledge-
ment of the information given by the teacher.

There is no room for closely guarded secrets when working in a
collaborative manner. Part of the role of a specialist worker must be
to enhance and develop skills in others. Therefore in-service training
and regular consultation should be an integral part of the support
offered by those with specialist skills.

The exchange of information, whether in the written or verbal
form should be shared with ease and confidence. As with all
communication, it is essential that what is said is understood by all
who hear/receive it. (For further discussion about communication
see the chapter about working in teams.) It is advisable that the main
points of any discussion are immediately written down as part of the
record keeping system. All technical/specialist words should be
explained in terms understood by the lay person. Then there can be
no misunderstandings created by jargon.

Example
Confusion over the term 'hypotonic' (floppy), was caused
when the visiting physiotherapist used it to describe a child's
muscle tone. The teacher thought she said 'hypertonic' (stiff)
and, not wanting to appear ignorant, did not ask for
clarification. When the teacher looked up the word
'hypertonic' in a medical dictionary she got completely the
opposite information about the child because it stated that
'hypertonic is excessive stiffness'. Writing in an annual review
that the child was very stiff did not give the parents the
impression that the teacher knew the child, or had talked with
the physio. The physiotherapist in turn was furious at being
misquoted.

Within a collaborative team, members should feel confident to ask for clarification of terminology, because it is easy to lose credibility when using terms not fully understood.

Aubrey (1990) states that it is often more difficult to develop credibility between two people of the same profession. This was confirmed by Thomas (1992) whose research found that teams of professionals with the same status – homogeneous teams – experienced more conflicts than heterogeneous teams. These would be made up of professionals from different disciplines and/or a mixture of volunteers and those of a different status. Teachers find it relatively easy to accept and act upon information and recommendations made by medical personnel or social services staff, whereas the suggestions made by support staff from education are sometimes harder to accept.

When working in the role of a support teacher, be it in a direct teaching mode of delivery or as an advisory service member employing a more indirect form of support, it takes a great deal of time to establish credibility. Many class teachers would prefer support staff to withdraw the children and work on a one to one basis outside the classroom setting thus allowing the class teacher to 'get on with teaching the rest of the class'. Several learning support staff offer to teach the class while the class teacher works closely with the children who have learning difficulties. By offering this form of role reversal support each person gains a deeper understanding of the situation and any limitations.

Internal support staff have a greater chance of developing credibility if they are seen to class teach for part of the week. The teacher in charge of resource based provision for the visually impaired in a large comprehensive school defends the policy that all specialist teachers working in that school class teach for 50 per cent of the week. One of the frequent criticisms of external support staff is their perceived inability to relate their knowledge to different situations – especially the large class setting.

There will be difficulty initiating a collaborative approach when the class teacher and the support service teacher have directly opposing views about teaching strategies, discipline and general pedagogy. Garnett (1988) poses the question of the management of classroom order and discipline when the member of support staff is present. Many special needs co-ordinators and advisory teachers are experienced members of staff who have posts of responsibility and a certain level of authority which is recognised by pupils and staff alike. It is therefore very intimidating for a newly qualified, or junior member of staff to teach in front of such support teachers. The fear of being judged by one's own profession can lead to resentment and a lack of ownership of the education of the children with learning difficulties (Thomas 1992). Garnett goes on to state that the delicate subject of discipline must be the responsibility of the regular teacher and that it should be discussed sensitively.

A poorly taught lesson and badly controlled class not only creates difficulties for the class/subject teacher, it also places the support teacher in a very embarrassing situation. The anguish described by Thomas in 'Extracts from the diary of a support teacher', as the chemistry lesson with a group of Year 9 pupils deteriorates, has been experienced by many specialist teachers. We have collected other examples:

Further examples
'My professional integrity would not allow me to take over when I first became aware that the subject teacher was losing control, however, when I realised that some of the less boisterous pupils were looking towards me to discipline those throwing objects around the room, then I felt it was time to intervene' – Head of special needs support, an inner city comprehensive.

'As the lesson went on and the children became more uninterested and restless I felt increasingly more embarrassed. She was obviously ill prepared and talked in terms clearly not understood by the majority of the class. If only I had been told that we would be looking at simple circuits I could have taken in my daughter's toy rabbit which is operated by a big switch that creates a simple circuit.' – Peripatetic teacher of the deaf, describing her feelings while supporting a couple of Year 4 children with hearing impairments.

The question of whether support should be provided by subject specialists or special needs specialists is one which can create heated discussion. The difficulties experienced by the special needs teacher who is timetabled to give support in a subject which they have not studied since their own school days can in turn cause embarrassment and it is questionable if such inadequate assistance is of any value. On the other hand the subject specialist who gives support must have the skills to adapt the materials and be fully aware of the diverse needs of each child.

Size of caseload

> Example
> The education authority of a large city undertook a review of its special needs provision during the Autumn Term 1989 and Spring Term 1990. As a result of the review, and in response to the Elton Report (1989), a Behaviour Support Service was developed with a head of service appointed in January 1991. By the end of the Autumn Term that year there had been 391 referrals to the service.

Such large numbers of referrals are not uncommon when services are created. Many services do not appear to reduce the numbers to manageable levels because many have the desire to support all referrals and hold the belief that large caseloads reflect their level of commitment.

Regular and consistent support is more difficult to achieve when unrealistic caseloads are given to support services. Caseloads of over 150 between four staff are not uncommon for specialist teachers. The stress caused by such large caseloads has been investigated by MacConville (1991). Many services do not have a strict criteria for intervention and find it difficult to say 'no' to casual referrals made while visiting a school. Without a policy which outlines the correct referral system and the criteria by which levels of intervention are agreed, services can be racing around without giving the appropriate level of support to those children who should come under their remit. Schools need to feel confident that they are getting 'value for money' and that the support will be regular. They should not be under the impression that the support teacher is there for a quick solution (Bowers, 1989). At the end of the initial contact the type and frequency of support should be outlined to the school and a contract drawn up which is agreed by all those involved with the child. (For further discussion about contracts see p.71.)

Special needs support teams within schools may consist of any number of staff. The people who make up the team often work part time and therefore meetings to discuss strategies and approaches, and to allocate workloads are sometimes hurried. If up to 18 per cent of the children in a school may experience learning difficulties

(Warnock, 1978), then the work of the co-ordinator in deciding who should be supported, the type of support and the frequency of that support will be a time consuming decision. Such decisions will require a whole school policy.

Status of the support service

Frequently, factors that create a good impression with schools are the job title of the support service staff and their status. This 'Legitimate credibility' (Davies and Davies, 1988) can influence initial contact with a school. The teachers of a city hospital school, who are involved in working with chronically sick children in the mainstream setting, all have the title of head in their role. Their consultancy role has been enhanced and schools are more willing to discuss at senior management level, the re-integration of such children. Aubrey (1990) states that the Consultant should be part of the senior management team and be regarded with equal standing.

> Example
> A speech therapist, Miss Fuller, had been asked to assess a child, Peter Shaw, with a view to submitting advice to the Statementing Officer. An appointment with the school had been made over the telephone and parents informed. When Miss Fuller arrived at the school she was kept waiting for half an hour. When she eventually saw the head teacher she was promptly informed that Peter had gone on a class outing. It was not surprising that after this visit a strong letter of complaint was written to the school head with a copy to the inspector for that school. The lack of respect for another professional's time perhaps would not have occurred had Miss Fuller had the title 'Head' or 'Advisor'.

The debate surrounding the status of support services will be ongoing. Conway (1989) discusses the difference between support teachers who are seen as 'experts' and those who are regarded as peers with common professional and career interests. The question remains − should the specialist knowledge held by support staff be considered worthy of a higher status than the generalist knowledge of the class teacher?

Outreach teachers based in schools for children with moderate learning difficulties have reported that they find their job much easier in a school where the special needs co-ordinator is someone with the time and status to liaise and then act upon the information given. Lloyd-Smith and Sinclair-Taylor (1988) outline some of the characteristics required by the person appointed to the role of special needs co-ordinator. If such a post holder is to be effective at all levels of management and with the governors and parents then the characteristics and skills such as:

- 'well qualified',
- 'advisor',
- 'course organiser',
- 'consultant',
- 'provider of effective support',

can only be expected if the correct level of pay and status is given to the post or further training offered.

Status across disciplines

In the report *Educational Provision for the Under Fives* by the House of Commons Select Committee (1989), closer collaboration between members of the 'rectangle of service providers' is recommended to provide various forms of pre-school education. The report clearly recognises that the difference in pay, status and conditions experienced by the professionals who work with young children can be a major obstacle. This obstacle is one of which team members must be aware and which is very apparent in all settings where there are children experiencing difficulties of learning and receiving support from various disciplines.

This major 'stumbling block' has been described by many collaborative team members. Status involves the standing of an individual based on qualifications and position in the community (Hunt, 1979). Broad differences within a group tend to reduce interaction and the support offered by team members. Given a typical team which gives support to a child and family, those with higher ranking positions, such as paediatricians and educational psychologists, will contribute and participate more frequently in case conferences and meetings. This can create frustrations amongst those of a lower status who are not so confident to speak out. Within the cross discipline training suggested in Chapter 7, an observer of role play meetings can note the frequency of participation by the various team members and present the findings for discussion.

Living a nomadic existence

The stresses of working in different situations cannot be overlooked. Peripatetic support staff have to be aware of the management and social structures within schools and organisations if they are to work effectively. Knowing the policies and procedures of each establishment and any hidden agenda can be the fine line between success or failure in a school.

Examples

1. Ms Kaur, a teacher of English as a Second Language, created quite a stir when she asked the school secretary for some stationary. Ms Kaur visited the school every Thursday to work with eight different children. On the Thursday morning in question she had planned to make some mobiles. Stationary in King's Street Primary School was always distributed on the first Tuesday of every month following a written request to the deputy. There was much resentment as the deputy was asked for the paper and crayons during his lunch break! The deputy felt that Ms Kaur's service should provide all the materials required. He also informed her that if she required further resources she should have written a list which could then been approved by the school head.

2. June Saunders, the visiting physiotherapist at Queensway Infant School was disliked by many of the staff because at break time she used any clean mug for her coffee and she sat in a different seat each week. All the staff had their own mug and always sat in the same chair in the staffroom. No one said anything to June, in fact they avoided engaging in conversation with her. The staff expected her to realise the procedures in their staffroom – thinking that such procedures were common to all schools.

The fact that a class teacher is reluctant to meet after school to discuss a child may be totally unrelated to their commitment to children with special needs, or linked with their dislike of working with another person. It may be simply that they are making a statement to their head teacher about the number of after school meetings they are expected to attend.

When staff are feeling uncertain about their posts, sensitivity is required. For example, when a school is due to be amalgamated with another and all staff have to apply for a post, then someone with a secure job may be resented. By being aware of tensions and pressures within certain schools, support staff can avoid making comments which could be classed as tactless.

The ability to analyse various situations, to know about the organisation of resources, to understand the management structure and financial priorities, are not easy skills to develop. To know, in practical terms the layout of the school, the storing of technical resources and the timing of sessions can all create an air of efficiency. To arrive at a school or meeting on time gains credibility whereas someone who is seen as 'arriving at anytime during the morning depending on any domestic crisis' may not be taken as seriously as someone who makes appointments and keeps to them.

To gain knowledge about the ethos and structure of a school takes time and effort as each will be unique to every establishment. At the same time as this practical knowledge is being gained, the support teacher has to become aware of which staff share the same philosophies. There appear to exist two groups of teachers:

1. those who feel that children progress more rapidly when they receive tuition on a withdrawal basis;
2. those who believe in the same education for all.

Clearly the teachers who see withdrawal as the answer to meeting special needs will not welcome collaborative working within their classroom.

The differences in policies from school to school is something of which support service personnel need to be aware and to accept. There is nothing more unprofessional than to criticise aspects of one school to staff of another.

Example
An assessment team was created in response to SATs at key stage one. It consisted of four teachers who went around the LEA working with staff to develop procedures for teacher assessment and the administering of SATs. After the initial visit by one of the team several school co-ordinators got together to discuss the outcome. It became clear that the seconded teacher had criticised at least one thing about the previous schools visited. Such behaviour did little to enhance the reputation of the team and it is not surprising that her contract was not renewed for a further year.

Personal characteristics and qualities

Take any cross section of society and it can be seen that some people are not 'team people'. There are some loners in all the support services who find it difficult to work with others. It is very stressful for such people to be put in the situation where they are expected to be part of a team. There are diverse opinions about the possible solutions when such a situation arises. One view is that people who are not naturally 'team people' can be 'counselled' and supported so they become team members. The alternative view is that these people are unlikely to make good team members if they are very reluctant. Their feelings and views should be accepted and respected.

It is suggested that support staff need four characteristics which will make them effective members of a collaborative team:

- skills;
- knowledge;
- experience;
- 'innate qualities'.

Skills can be developed through training. Knowledge and experience can be gained over time. While the fourth characteristic, which we have termed an 'innate quality', is something which not all people possess and yet is vital for effective team membership. This 'innate quality' can be defined as the ability to work with others and to be aware of the value of contributions others can make to a situation.

Example
Reorganisation of a service for children with sensory impairments created the situation where two members of staff were going into one primary school. Each was responsible for a key stage within the National Curriculum. The head of the school questioned why one member of the service was welcomed while the other was avoided, with staff reluctant to arrange meetings for discussion. The staff informed the head that one member of the team valued their opinions, respected their views, worked with them in deciding teaching strategies and long term goals. She always produced the information or equipment promised and arrived at the stated time and worked with the child when it was felt to be appropriate. The other member of the support service usually arrived late, was very rushed and unprepared, always made negative statements

about the materials produced by the class teacher or non teaching assistant and had failed to produce a written report during the eight months of 'support'.

On closer analysis of the above situation, it can be noted that both support service staff had a wealth of experience and knowledge, both had the skills to carry out their job but the innate qualities to work as a member of a team, to communicate effectively with the aim of sharing and enabling were not within the one teacher's capabilities. It can be argued, that what the ineffective teacher lacked were skills which could be trained. The opportunity to develop the skills could be part of her development programme highlighted during appraisal. Running alongside the courses could be support discussions by the head of service and the tightening of procedures to ensure better time keeping, etc. Can the characteristic to co-operate be developed through training? Can the interpersonal skills required to work with others be gained through courses or can it be argued that courses can only enhance qualities already present?

Example

Miss Simons is a teacher of children with severe learning difficulties. She has a calm, quiet manner which has proved very successful with children who have challenging behaviour. Unfortunately Miss Simons is unable to work as an equal member of a team. She usually feels inferior and lacks the skills to assert her authority as a class teacher. As a consequence the nursery nurse attached to her class takes long coffee breaks and decides the jobs she will undertake and the children with whom she will work. According to the nursery nurse, Mrs Bell, Miss Simons is ineffective, lacking in direction and not much fun to work alongside. Both have very good skills with the pupils, but appear to be unable to work together for the benefit of the children. Miss Simons and Mrs Bell were not given any encouragement, time or opportunity to discuss their different philosophies. So their differences grew and their self concepts shattered. It seems unfortunate that such skilful people were not encouraged to use their skills in a complementary, collaborative manner.

Team membership

Collaborative teams that are formed to support children with difficulties in learning do not always consist of people one would choose to work alongside. In industry personnel officers are increasingly administering personality tests to applicants with the aim of discovering if they will make good team members. The Myers-Briggs Type Indicator is one such test which, after completing a given questionnaire, indicates personality type. This will be either

- extroversion or introversion;
- sensing or intuition;
- thinking or feeling;
- judging or perceiving.

Teams in industry have to be finely balanced and are created generally to increase productivity or sales. If all members of the team are predominantly extrovert the team would not necessarily develop and achieve joint goals. Our chapter which looks at effective team building will examine membership of various teams and the balance for which to aim.

Support staff will be members of many different teams and therefore may undertake team building exercises with their immediate colleagues but not with the various people with whom they will come into contact. While most heads of services and schools will try to avoid personality clashes there can never be a guarantee that the team will 'gel'. The only safeguard can be general training in the skills required to work alongside others and specific training for team members who will work together regularly.

Communication skills

In order to work effectively as a team there have to be agreed goals and objectives. When problems arise there must be an open forum where each member of the team can discuss any difficulties experienced. Communication should increase when there are problems so that solutions can be found. Gilmore *et al.* (1974) in their studies of health teams discovered that the most commonly adopted method of dealing with difficulties was to reduce communication between team members. This is frequently the case where there is conflict between the special needs support staff and the class teacher. When caseloads are large it is convenient to reduce visits to a school where relationships are not harmonious. This avoids further conflict.

There may be several reasons why this evasion of any attempt to problem solve or resolve conflicts appears to be commonplace in the field of special education. One reason could be that people are unable to differentiate between interpersonal and inter professional relations. There frequently appears to be a problem for some teachers who cannot accept that a colleague can be a nice person but not very good at their job. Due to the lack of appropriate training a disagreement about certain strategies, or the use of a particular piece of equipment, can too often be taken as a personal criticism. Conflict can be healthy for a team in that it can make various members question their practice. It should not be taken as an index of failure for the team to work together. The common, negative view of conflicts can cause unnecessary energy to be channelled into avoiding discussion and there is a danger that maintaining harmonious relationships can become an end in itself rather than being regarded as a means of achieving better quality service for children with special needs.

Thomas (1992) refers to Wilson (1989) who explored the need to ensure team members have:

- consultation skills,
- counselling skills,
- negotiation skills,

in order to reduce the misunderstandings and tensions which can frequently occur when there are two, or more, professionals working in a classroom. It is considered that the above skills equip team members to enter into discussions without using language which can be misinterpreted as being a personal criticism. For further discussion see Chapter 6.

The lack of training to work collaboratively — for class and subject teachers

In order to provide a broad, balanced and differentiated curriculum relevant to the needs of each child *all* staff must be able to recognise when a child has special needs and know who they can contact for specialist help and advice. This has been one of the main emphases of training over the past ten years. The skills then required to maximise help and advice given has not featured so prominently. For there to be an effective partnership between professionals and across disciplines working co-operatively is essential. The opportunity to pool ideas and expertise should be available.

> Example
> A group of twenty special needs co-ordinators were asked to identify the number of professionals who visited their school. On average the co-ordinators liaise with between nine and thirteen different visiting professionals. The educational psychologist being the person listed by all. When asked if they were aware of the training received by these professionals, the majority stated that although they had some information mainly about the courses available, they were unaware of the course content and the exit competencies.

If members of the collaborative team have expectations of each other's role and skills which are in accord with reality then there will be few problems. If there are serious discrepancies then considerable difficulties may arise. The expectations can be shaped by more information which in turn can be gained through joint training.

Lack of training for – specialists

The specialist courses presently available cover the skills and competencies required to teach and work with children with a particular special educational need. There does appear to be a distinct lack of management skills as an integral part of courses. The skills required to work collaboratively namely:

- negotiating skills,
- communication and interpersonal skills,
- time and case management,
- the organisation of meetings and case conferences,
- report writing and record keeping,
- influencing change as a member of a visiting support service,

are hardly touched upon in most specialist courses. Yet these are essential for effective collaborative working. Such is the emphasis placed upon these skills that our chapter about training will examine these in more detail. Dean (1992) in her handbook for inspectors, advisers and advisory teachers discusses the importance of these skills when in an advisory role and adds that there is a lack of relevant courses presently available to develop such skills.

The specialist, segregated nature of the educational preparation of the various professionals providing the services to identified pupils and their families can hinder teamwork. The specialist nature of the training can provide a limited view of facilities and provision. Jargon, along with ideologies and values which are different for each discipline can cause barriers to understanding by those professionals outside that particular discipline. Strauss (1962) remarked

> professionalism complicates the task of developing teamwork between occupations. Each profession tends to develop a parochial specialised point of view. As a result, jurisdictional disputes become common and the overall system starts to break down into a number of semi-autonomous departments.

We believe that as long as specialist training is carried out in isolation collaborative working will be more difficult to achieve and therefore it will take longer before children and their families benefit from a more cohesive joint approach. If each specialist course contained an element of cross-discipline training then collaboration would be a more natural process rather than something feared due to unfamiliarity.

Lack of whole school policies

Ainscow and Florek (1989) define a whole school approach to meeting the diverse needs of pupils as one where 'attempts are being made to utilise all the resources of a school to foster the development of all its children' (p.3).

When a special needs policy has been developed in a school without consultation with all the staff, there will be little or no ownership. Thomas and Jackson (1989) emphasise the fact that the organisation of schools is complex and can easily become unbalanced. They support the need to involve all staff at various stages of project development and present a seven phase outline of the introduction, induction and implementation of a project where the staff of the remedial department took on a whole school role:

- Phase 1 – Fact finding
- Phase 2 – Regular feedback to senior management
- Phase 3 – Seeking opinions of staff

- Phase 4 – Presentation
- Phase 5 – Giving the innovation status
- Phase 6 – Maintenance
- Phase 7 – Practice

(Thomas and Jackson, 1989, pp.11–14)

Lack of an appropriate base

Effective service delivery may be hampered by the lack of an appropriate base. Even if teams are adequately trained and prepared for working in an interdependent manner they will experience difficulties in following through their ideas if environmental or administrative factors are lacking. The type and quality of housing for support services varies from Local Authority to Local Authority and within Authorities (HMI, 1989).

> Examples
> A. For three years a peripatetic support service was housed in a hut which had been declared unfit for use by children. The roof leaked, the drains frequently became blocked and the heating system was inefficient. The LEA was fully aware of these difficulties but did not urgently seek an alternative base because of the itinerant nature of the service.

In some cases services have a suitable base but lack the correct facilities.

> B. One sensory support service does not have clerical support and listed this as *the* biggest stumbling block to their efficiency. A survey of six sensory services consisting of between five and fifteen staff revealed that the number of clerical hours varied from none to thirty-five hours per week with an average of twelve.

The use of precious resources in school based provision can be a source of friction.

> C. The secretary of the school where an itinerant service was based was not allowed to take messages for the support staff because of the time involved. The service were not given a direct line or answering machine. The resulting impression, gained by parents and other professionals, was of a service which could not be contacted.

Sharing a base with other support services can provide the opportunity to develop an efficient system of communication and joint training. The central location of services enables informal contact on a regular basis which in turn can reduce status differences and increase communication. As one physiotherapist stated, 'it is much easier and quicker to solve problems and to clarify information if you are in close contact with other support staff'. A consultant ophthalmologist also stated, 'it is much more difficult to be rude to someone if you see them regularly'. However, the physical separateness from the schools may be regarded as an additional factor which distances the support staff from the 'chalk-face' and must be a factor taken into consideration when looking at long term policies.

One current argument is that support services are distanced by the creation of separate bases with separate heads of service. The services are seen as empires which fuel the barrier between mainstream and special education. Some educationalists are of the opinion that specialists should be school based with direct responsibility to the head teacher. In this way children with diverse needs would be viewed as part of a continuum, not separate and special. The debate continues.

General finance and resources

In order to offer effective support, support services in turn need to be given support (Davies and Davies, 1988).

> Example
> Out of fifteen services contacted only one service head felt that their budget for general resources was adequate. The head in question was quick to point out that this was perhaps because all major items had been purchased in previous years and consequently no substantial expenditure was envisaged. All the heads stated that their services were generally under resourced, especially in the area of IT.

In-service training budgets for support services were described as 'grossly inadequate' by twelve heads of service who were inter-viewed. The average allowance per teacher being approximately £70. The specialist service heads emphasised the need for their staff to keep up to date with national developments within their own specialism in addition to general educational progress.

Example
The identified £70 would not pay for a teacher in Manchester to attend a course in London if peaktime travel was required for instance. Although many courses can be attended within the locality — 'in-house' INSET — there is a danger of losing touch with the national overview.

External administration demands

Bowers (1991a) has stated that over the period of four years, 1987–1991, 78 statutory documents were issued by the Ministers of Education and the DES (now the DFE). The amount of information contained in the circulars and memoranda can be overwhelming for many and yet it is essential that support services be aware of the content and the implications for their work. The amount of literature which has been produced since the Education Reform Act 1988 has proved daunting. Ministers of Education appear to want to make their particular marks and as a consequence more circulars are issued and require careful consideration as sections which supersede earlier ones are examined.

LMS — Local Management of Schools

With the introduction of Local Management of Schools with its delegated budgets schools have become more aware of the cost of different services. It can be envisaged that schools will buy in services for certain pupils with special needs, but not necessarily for the majority of pupils who do not have the protection of a Statement of Special Educational Needs. Dyson (1990) points out that special needs co-ordinators in secondary schools are not viewed by their colleagues as being directly responsible for a class of pupils and could therefore be 'dispensable'.

Those involved in special education feel generally vulnerable, especially when there are reports of support service posts being frozen. There is a general feeling that special needs is a low priority area which is currently out of vogue. With the publication of result tables being a legal requirement, schools will not welcome children whose diverse needs will prevent them from reaching the average level of attainment. The only support service which will be welcomed will be the psychological service as schools refer children for assessment under the 1981 Education Act with the ultimate aim of getting a Statement of Special Educational Needs which will, in turn, either identify guaranteed additional resources or the transfer to a special school.

Support across the curriculum

In a recent speech by the Chairman of the National Curriculum Council, David Pascall, the question of subject specialists to teach key stage 2 was discussed. Teachers comment that the National Curriculum is proving to be too complex and prescriptive. The support teacher who has a caseload which covers all age and ability ranges will not feel secure in providing differentiated material at all levels. If breadth and balance are to be retained then support services will require additional time to work alongside mainstream staff in the attempt to give full curriculum access to pupils with diverse needs. The implications therefore should not be a reduction in service personnel but an increase.

The second part of the book will examine some of the practical ways in which support services can work collaboratively with mainstream staff to provide a whole curriculum which fulfils the demands of the Education Reform Act.

Lack of time

This 'stumbling block' is identified as a major problem by all support staff. Whenever new initiatives are suggested staff will invariably state:

- 'There just isn't enough time.'
- 'How can we support all the children on our caseload when there are only 24 hours in a day?'
- 'When have I got time to write up the information about the children I support?'
- 'I haven't got time to get involved in this new project.'
- 'When can I make time to visit the consultant to discuss these new referrals?'

Effective team building, the development of collaborative working strategies and all the skills required to work efficiently as a team initially take time to develop. This initial investment of time is considered crucial for the foundation stones to be set. How can this time be justified when caseloads are large and the curricular demands heavy? Support staff have frequently aimed to set aside time to exchange information with the key personnel involved with the child or young person they support. However, there has been very little timetabled time in the early stages of involvement in order to observe the class teacher's methods of working. The time taken to break down barriers, when the team membership is initially identified, is time well spent and should be organised using a recognised time management method.

Time management courses may cover:

- the principles
    - the basics of time management
    - time controllers
    - the benefits of better time utilisation
    - prime time
    - setting priorities
- time management techniques
    - planning
    - long term planning
    - short term planning
    - daily plans
    - characteristics of good planners
    - common time wasters
    - dealing with time wasters
    - tips for effective time management
- Action plans   (Haynes, 1987)

If time management courses are to be effective, and the techniques implemented, then all members of a team should attend such courses and an agreed planning format adopted. With so many challenges and demands upon our valuable time, effective organisation and planning is a must for all support staff.

After reading the 'stumbling blocks' listed above it may seem surprising that any services offer the type of effective support which we know currently exists. The determination of some support personnel to meet the needs of the pupils and their families is acknowledged. The lack of adequate resources has been a feature of the education of children with diverse needs for the last twelve years. In the present economic climate it is unlikely that this will improve. There are, however, some factors which can be seen as 'starting blocks' and as such can be used to create more effective support – these will be discussed in the next chapter.

CHAPTER 3

Starting Blocks

In this chapter there will be an outline of some of the 'starting blocks' which have helped to raise the status of support services and 'starting blocks' which can be used to aid service development. The factors discussed in the different sections provide the opportunity for collaborative working to support access to the whole curriculum for pupils with diverse needs. Throughout this chapter issues will be highlighted which can be debated by support staff as they aim to provide a service which is effective, efficient and appropriate for the 1990s.

Although this chapter is mainly about peripatetic services, much of the discussion could be applicable to in-house support within schools and services from other disciplines.

Recent legislation

Some recent legislation has created opportunities for support services to develop. Requests to support children with diverse needs to gain access to the curriculum have been numerous and services are continuing to develop and expand. Currently several Local Education Authorities, in response to The Elton Report (DES, 1989), have created services for primary aged children with emotional and behavioural difficulties. The aims of such services are to provide support for the child and to work proactively with schools in order to prevent pupil expulsion. Schools welcome such intervention and are eager to co-operate with these services.

Education Reform Act 1988

a) National Curriculum
The National Curriculum has helped to raise expectations of pupils who experience difficulties in learning. A broad and balanced

curriculum has given pupils more opportunities and a greater chance to succeed. Several mainstream schools are making positive links with special schools. The thematic approach developed in programmes of study to cover National Curriculum subjects at key stage 1, offer common areas where children can work together, each at different levels within the topic.

Since the introduction of the National Curriculum there has developed a common language between special schools, support service staff and mainstream teachers. The mainstream thinking which has now been adopted by special schools has been of tremendous help to outreach teachers who work in mainstream schools for part of their timetable. Joint in-service training for teachers working with children at key stages 1 and 2 has provided the opportunity for the exchange of ideas with regard to teaching approaches and record keeping. The establishment of joint working relationships have demonstrated the advantages of seeking common ground and the National Curriculum provides such opportunities (Ashdown *et al.*, 1991).

b) Local Management of Schools
Local Management of Schools has been listed as a 'stumbling block' and discussed in the previous chapter, but it can also be viewed as a 'starting block'. As 'market-led' forces become more prominent in education, services will be forced to take stock of their current position and develop strategies to respond to changing needs.

The preparations which support services should be undertaking to ensure survival with future delegation are discussed below.

After delegated budgets

In-service

The training days which are now a formal part of each teacher's year are considered a 'starting block' towards meeting the diverse needs of pupils across the whole curriculum. In order to heighten the awareness of mainstream staff who may be required to work with a cross section of children with special needs, in-service training packages have been developed by many support services. The training has been presented to staff not only to increase their knowledge of diverse needs, but also to cover possible teaching approaches. The Special Needs Action Programme (SNAP) packages developed in Coventry in the early 1980s had this initial aim (Muncey and Ainscow, 1983).

The fact that the majority of schools have special needs co-ordinators is a major 'starting block'. This has enabled support services to make initial contacts and offer in-service training for all mainstream staff. The training days have proved to be a golden opportunity for support services to make themselves known to schools and to describe their role. Many services, recognising the power of school governors have included them in awareness training.

Over the past ten years there has been a growing awareness that no one person can have the skills to support the cross section of children with special needs that one might find in a mainstream school. It is the special needs co-ordinator's responsibility to gather information about the diverse area of special needs. It is impossible for that person to know everything there is to know about various physical and sensory impairments, in addition to learning difficulties. Therefore special needs co-ordinators are seen as the link person for the specialist support services and the gatherers of information about the services available. The information which the co-ordinators collate will only be as good as the information they are given by the support services. Such information must outline the quality and scope of service on offer. Booklets/leaflets and videos can be produced as part of a marketing plan and would be seen as part of a promotional initiative.

Marketing

The majority of work cited in this section is by Bowers who has been at the forefront of research and developments in this area. His publications constitute the majority of materials available and some have been used to form the basis of the suggestions presented.

Marketing should be viewed as a 'starting block'. With the implementation of the Education Reform Act support services must carry out an audit and explore marketing strategies (Bowers, 1991b). The audit should be an examination of the stage of development of the service at the present time, the strengths of each member of the team and the factors which will influence how the service can progress. Such an audit will serve to influence the creation of a service plan and a staff development policy. These will help to highlight and target identified gaps in the service. Through creating a policy document, based partly upon the surveyed needs of 'customers' and the audit, a service should be able to offer support for the whole age range and to meet the complete continuum of needs within their specialism. For example, the situation of an advisory service employing initially trained primary staff who do not feel comfortable working within the secondary sector could be avoided. In-built evaluation of service delivery linked to appraisal is an effective way of guaranteeing that staff keep up to date and offer the type of service which meets the needs of the children, their teachers and families.

Marketing services which schools will buy in, may be viewed with distaste by many (MacConville, 1991), but it is a reality. Literature produced by the service can make schools aware of the need for the specialist skills on offer. Many schools are unaware of the various skills many support staff possess as the areas covered in their specialist training are not widely known. The visiting support person can often be viewed as having only narrow skills. It took the attendance at a national conference for a class teacher to understand fully the wide variety of roles undertaken by the specialist teacher for the visually impaired who made weekly visits to her classroom.

It is worth noting that in the field of visual impairment and multi-sensory impairment, voluntary agencies were the first to provide support for children who were visually impaired (the RNIB) or deaf – blind (SENSE) and schools were grateful for the help and advice given. The type of support offered varied from close collaboration with the family, 'hands-on' work with the child and consultancy work with staff. The frequency of visits also varied according to need. When one of these agencies decided to ask LEAs for a contribution to the costs incurred, many LEAs did not respond. Several authorities decided to try to employ their own teachers to carry out the specialist work while others asked for details of how the voluntary agency had been offering support.

Many questions can be asked as a result of this information.

- Under LMS will cluster schools employ a generic special educationalist?
- Will children be integrated without the correct level of specialist support?
- Will independent consultants spring up like daisies after a spring shower?
- Will voluntary agencies decide that this is the growth area in which they wish to become more actively involved?

- Will those children without the protection of a Statement of Special Educational Needs be given any additional support?

It is not too early for support staff to review their practice. To examine the costs incurred in providing an efficient support service for various children is more difficult than it may first appear. It is not easy to state the real costs which include direct and indirect costings.

Direct costs are easier to calculate because they include:

- equipment;
- consumables;
- telephone and postage;
- travel;
- in-service training;
- the salaries of the service staff.

Indirect costs are harder to identify and to calculate. They include:

- the heating and lighting of a building;
- the furniture;
- services such as cleaning and decorating.

The first step in working out the costs would be to examine the work of the team in great detail, to identify the time spent in each school and to state all the resources involved in that visit.

It is normal practice within services to have various intervention categories. For example:

Category 1 — those children who receive daily support;
Category 2 — weekly support;
Category 3 — monthly support;
Category 4 — termly support;
Category 5 — yearly review visits.

The true costs of each category will include *time* for:

- working directly with the child;
- material adaptations;
- discussion with the class teacher, parents and head of the school;
- telephone calls to arrange visits and gather information;
- report writing;
- travelling to and from base to school.

In addition there will be the hidden costs and general running costs. *Costs* such as:

- telephone rental;
- stationery;
- secretarial time;
- word-processing facilities;
- heating and lighting.

Support services are currently 'free' so referrals come thick and fast – and caseloads are generally huge. This almost certainly will not be the case when schools have to buy in support. There has been an increase in the number of referrals for statements since the introduction of delegated budgets, noted by Bowers (1991b), which may be some indication that schools want a guarantee of regular support and additional resources. With the present system of support for children with diverse needs pupils can receive specialist input without a statement. However, with Local Management of Schools and the reduction in the budget for special needs, support staff may only become involved on a regular basis when a statement has been written.

Booth *et al.* (1992) describe the 1990 survey of Local Education Authorities by the Special Educational Needs National Advisory Council (SENNAC). The LEAs that replied saw a place for support services in the future. In the same chapter the unpublished work of Lincoln (1991) is cited. Lincoln questioned the views of schools with regard to Special Educational Needs Support Services and came to the conclusion that there were serious doubts about their long term survival. Schools did not want individual tuition, they would only buy in-service training and advice in developing whole school initiatives.

In Chapter 2 we gave the account of how two people became heads of a peripatetic service by default. Management skills had to be learnt as the services developed. In the current economic climate heads of support services will not only need effective management skills but also marketing skills. Such as:

- market awareness
- identification of clients
- legal limitations
- marketing components
- reaching the market

68

- developing a marketing plan
- promotional strategies
- selling

(Bowers, 1991b, pp.106–34)

If heads make a conscious decision not to develop such skills personally then they should identify a member of the team to lead or co-ordinate marketing and to receive and provide appropriate training. This should be considered when designing the service development plan and should be seen as part of the *team's* professional development. Bowers (1991b) puts great emphasis on the need for all members of the service to be responsible for marketing and states that the alternative to marketing is 'decline or extinction' (p.108). He points out that although the term 'marketing' conjures up a picture of advertising and selling these are only part of the whole process. 'Systematic impression management' is considered to be fundamental and consists of the *whole* of the potential market being given a favourable picture of the services' functioning (p.114).

When trying to decide who the 'customers or recipients' will be support services should be aware of the cross-discipline element. Bowers lists five groups of recipients:

- the *end-users* – those whom the service sets out to benefit
- the *deciders* – those who make the decision that the service is necessary or desirable
- the *influencers* – those who can encourage, modify or discourage the decision
- the *purchaser* – those who pay for the results of any decision
- the *gatekeeper* – who can grant or deny access to any or all of the above.

(Bowers, 1991b, p.109)

Each of these recipients has the same level of importance with varying powers and requiring different market processes. The recipients in the two categories of 'deciders' and 'influencers' may be members of other disciplines. For example the ophthalmologist or educational psychologist will decide whether a service is necessary and can influence the decision to buy in a service by directly stating the need and by discussion with parents. Collaborative working can therefore be viewed as valuable to the survival of support services. Other professionals are more likely to recommend a service with whom they have worked and for whom they have respect.

Marketing starts with market research − finding out what demand there is for an item or service, and what purchasers expect for their money. At the present time the main client of support services is the LEA. With delegated budgets this will shift − Circular 7/91 (DES, 1991) points out that 'from time to time schools should be able to exercise the option to use an alternative source of supply' (para.57).

What will schools expect when they are paying directly? Bowers describes various types of market research and the procedures involved:

- Distribution research − looking at ways in which services are organised and how they reach the users
- Service research − examining the client's (present and future) perception of the service
- Pricing research − which looks closely at the effects of different costs for different levels of service and in comparison with other services.
- Desk research − a generic form which encompasses all the research that gains new information.
- Internal audit − an objective look at present activities.

(Bowers, 1991b, p.124)

This final component Bowers feels is essential. The *internal audit* is an examination of the present position of a service, how it got there and where it aims to go in the future. A SWOT analysis, which looks at the Strengths, Weaknesses, Opportunities and Threats, could help in the internal audit process. (For further details see Chapter 6.)

Example of a learning support service SWOT
Strengths:
- four highly qualified and experienced members of staff;
- a clear policy document outlining the aims of the service;
- a criteria for intervention with well documented procedures for referrals;
- good links with associated personnel in health, social services and the local voluntary agencies;
- promotional literature about the service;
- a good reputation in the schools visited.

Weaknesses:
- all staff were initially primary trained;
- only four hours clerical support per week;
- large caseload with a 'waiting list';
- no IT for record and files.

Opportunities:
- marketing course available for education staff;
- training in IT to develop system of record keeping;
- INSET package developed by the team;
- The Children Act 1989 which calls for a register of Children in Need − an opportunity to collaborate with others;
- the National Curriculum for All requiring that all children have access to a common curriculum.

Threats?
- the reduced role of the Local Education Authority;
- Local Management of Schools and delegated budgets;
- special needs as being viewed as out of vogue.

Service agreements

Services should carry out a survey (audit) of the needs within their area (market research) confirming the type of service required by heads, governors, teachers and parents in addition to other disciplines. Linked with this they could make sure that their 'would-be customers' are aware of the skills within the service and the need for specialist approaches to provide a differentiated curriculum which meets each child's needs. The resulting document would lead to the 'service agreement' which Circular 7/91 para.56 (DES, 1991) envisages being a paper which specifies 'the scope, quality, duration and cost of the service to be provided'.

Although the circular only lists four components to the Service Agreement:

- scope
- quality
- duration
- cost

Bowers (1991a) has put forward twelve:

- description of the parties involved
- objectives of the agreement

- the timescale
- the services to be covered
- volume and mix − giving specified bands of service delivery depending upon needs
- existing involvement
- the price
- the terms of payment
- quality
- monitoring
- variations of service agreements and finally
- remedies for non-performance.

(Bowers, 1991a, pp.28−31)

The Service Agreement can be seen as a contract at the first tier level. The first part of the total package. At the present time it will be an agreement entered into by the support service and the LEA − this almost certainly will change in the near future.

Developing Contracts

One of the most important mechanisms for encouraging collaboration between services, and between services and schools is the development of Contracts. The type of support offered by various services can be vastly different from the type of support expected by schools. Many services over the past ten years have taken on an advising and consultancy role, employing an approach which is aimed at developing the skills of the class teacher who has daily contact with the child (see Chapter 1). Frequent complaints are centred around the fact that teachers expect support to be directed at pupils. Indirect consultancy has not always been the type of support expected by some staff:

'We expect visiting specialists to work directly with the child.'
'How can I carry out everything that is recommended when I have thirty other children to teach?'

are both comments written by mainstream teachers when asked to give their views about Special Needs Support Services.

Misunderstandings are frequently created with this type of support. As review and evaluation are often non-existent it can be difficult for schools and services to sort out these differences. The lack of collaborative discussion to develop a joint plan can create further friction. If there is an absence of frequent evaluation built into what support services offer and if continuity does not appear to be a major feature of service delivery, then schools will question if they are receiving a valuable resource. Class teachers and support personnel have all stated the frustration created when either the support member of staff has missed an arranged visit or the school has failed to inform the support service that the child is absent.

There is obviously a need for accountability on all sides. A contract appears to be the most appropriate way forward to achieve this. Some support services are unhappy about the formal term 'Contract', preferring to use the term 'Service Agreement'. This term may appear less formal but it also gives the impression of being one sided – the support service agreeing to provide a service without the balance of the other parties involved being committed in some way. It has been stated earlier that Service Agreements are the first process in a formal agreement. They are viewed as the process of 'laying out the stall' of what it has to offer. The Contract is the second tier, and is drawn up primarily between the support staff and the class teacher to clarify finer details once an agreement has been accepted by the 'purchaser'. The Contract is seen as a structured document which provides:

- an outline of what a service can offer;
- how and when the support will be delivered;
- what the intended outcome will be;
- how this will be evaluated;
- the time schedule;
- an outline of what facilities and information the school will provide;
- what type of backup work will be carried out between visits; and
- the general expectations of all.

At the time of Contract completion all (including parents and, where appropriate, the young person) should know exactly what the document contains and as a result should be left in no doubt as to their commitment to the Contract.

Several class and support service teachers have questioned the emergence of Contracts, stating that such formal procedures are not necessary. One experienced peripatetic teacher of the deaf articulated her displeasure at a 'restricting, rigid monitoring system'. Clough and Lindsay (1991) clearly demonstrate that Contracts are essential for effective service delivery. However, such procedures have to be introduced in an expedient manner. In the initial stages the head of the support service should negotiate with the head (or a member of the senior management team) of the school. Such discussions should not be left for support staff to initiate.

The most logical way forward would be:

- the head of service to call together the heads of the schools concerned and outline the rationale behind the change in service procedures. In this way general consensus of feeling towards the Contract could be judged and appropriate alterations made.
- A pilot project, with an identified time line, would enable those heads who were a little apprehensive about the system to try it out and contribute recommendations at the time of review.

For successful acceptance of new initiatives and an agreed approach to children with diverse needs a whole school policy has to be adopted (Hegarty, 1987). Contracts should be part of that policy.

Example
The service for children with sensory impairments in Treeshire decided, after undertaking a full audit, to develop Contracts between the service, schools, parents and pupils. The Head of the service, Mrs Mason, had involved the Local Education Authorities Inspector for Special Needs and a group of mainstream headteachers who were receiving regular support from her service. A draft Contract, developed by the whole service, was presented to the initial meeting of the steering committee. The redesigned document was then piloted for a term and evaluation comments used to make minor modifications. The support service were given a day's training which covered negotiation skills and methods to introduce Contracts into schools. Role play was a major part of the day with video recordings of face to face discussions.

The support staff were convinced that Contracts were the way forward and therefore felt confident about introducing the system into the schools. The schools had been prepared and involved in the initial stages therefore the project received the status and commitment required.

Such major and important changes warrant time and training. The support staff must feel convinced that the Contract system is the way forward and that it will benefit the children and contribute to the efficiency and survival of their service. These feelings cannot be engendered overnight, nor by suddenly producing a draft Contract. Our chapter on team work demonstrates that successful teams collaborate and consult at all key stages of development. Full and frank discussions enable the fears felt by those who have worked in a certain style for many years to be expressed and acknowledged.

Contracts can be seen as linking in with appraisal. During the appraisal meeting (which should be a two way system) identified in-service training needs may be highlighted as a direct result of the Contract system. Courses covering negotiating skills along with time and case management may be required so that realistic support can be written in the Contracts.

A working party is suggested, comprising a sample of all who are affected by the introduction of Contracts, to review the procedure through a systematic approach. In this way collaborative working can aid the development of a procedure which, it is felt, can offer an effective way forward for support services. Constant reviews should point the way forward. Bowers (1992) argues that a support service should not be at the same point of development three months hence. All support services should have clear policies of where they intend to be in the future, what they have to offer and their criteria for intervention. Without this clear, yet flexible vision there is a danger that support services will not use the present climate to their best advantage. Our final chapter, *Developing an Action Plan*, looks at the ways in which a clear vision for the future may be gained.

Whole school approach

The advantages of a whole school approach to meeting diverse needs of pupils is well documented (Bines, 1988; Dessent, 1988; Gordon, 1989). As senior management teams are becoming more skilful at management techniques and employ 'bottom up' methods of management in addition to the 'top down' system, then more schools are developing whole school policies to address certain issues. This type of policy development can create numerous opportunities for support services. In the chapter outlining the many difficulties facing support services in their plight to provide effective support the lack of a clear, agreed policy was listed. Willey (1989) in her article about the whole school approach concludes by outlining the positive effect such a policy has on pupil self-esteem and pupil interaction. Staff from support services would endorse this stating that it also has a positive effect upon staff interaction and collaboration.

The Children Act (1989)

Although on first examination The Children Act may not appear to be a factor which should be considered when discussing support services and the whole curriculum, on closer examination there are many implications which should be investigated.

The Children Act offers the tool for encouraging collaborative working across disciplines. Local Authorities have a duty under section 17(1) of the Act:

> to safeguard and promote the welfare of children within their area who are in need
> and
> so far as is consistent with that duty to promote the upbringing of such children by their families, by providing a range of services appropriate to the child's need.

According to section 17(5a) of the Act the Local Authority does not have to provide all the services needed by itself. In fact Local Authorities are charged with facilitating the provision by others including voluntary organisations. Collaborative working is the only way in which there can be a firm decision about the services needed by each family. Russell (1990) points out that co-ordinating the many services involved with children with disabilities will require time and resources in addition to the assessment of compatibility of services.

There is no doubt that there is a danger that support services (across the disciplines) will be underused, or will not be involved at the appropriate stage, unless they make themselves known to other services and parents. Local Authorities will be required to provide information about existing services. Therefore it is crucial that all relevant, jargon free, information about services involved with the assessment and planning for children with learning difficulties is made known to all concerned. The promotional materials mentioned earlier would serve this purpose. The Children Act uses the term 'local authority' and gives the impression that all departments and committees should develop an agreed strategy to implement the Act. Such a strategy would hinge upon collaborative working. As there were no additional resources linked with this Act (as with the 1981 Education Act), there must be joint assessment of need and joint assessment of local provision to meet identified needs. Such action would achieve maximum impact yet avoid duplication and waste.

> Example
> Jill Smale, a pre-school teacher for children with special needs went to visit Tony Brown, a four year old with a rare genetic disorder. Jill decided that she would like further information about Tony's communication skills and so took along *The Pragmatics Profile of Early Communication Skills* which would involve going through a profile checklist with Mrs Brown. Jill told Mrs Brown of her intention and as she produced the booklet out of her bag Mrs Brown laughed and explained that the speech therapist had spent two hours with her the day before covering the same information.

By linking in with health, social services and voluntary agencies, education support services can use the register of need, required by the Act, to move forward in developing a collaborative approach. Joint planning teams and working groups need to be set up to identify an effective way forward. Heads of services within education should not be slow to make approaches to equivalent post holders/counterparts within health and social services. The status differential should not be viewed as a barrier. There exists, at the present time, an awareness, by those working with children, of the need for interdependence by all services. This awareness is seen as a starting block.

Questions to ask

- How can the above be achieved?
- What kind of plan or agreement should be designed so that service providers can work together?
- Will the Service Audit and Service Agreements provide a clear focus of what can be achieved?

The call for collaborative working across disciplines is further strengthened by the Department of Health (1990) in *The Care of*

Children: Principles and Practice. In the *Regulations and Guidance* it states that:

> the various departments of a local authority (e.g. health, housing, education and social services) should co-operate to provide an integrated service and a range of resources even when such co-operation is not specifically required by law.

Are staff trained sufficiently to work in the collaborative manner expected by such regulations?

The same guidance also states: 'Co-operation between organisations, departments and individuals is crucial in the provision of protection for vulnerable children and also in ensuring proper use of available resources'.

Support services need to start planning collaborative strategies *now*.

Training

As we have devoted a whole chapter to training we will only touch upon the topic briefly in this section. Recent education publications are emphasising the need for collaboration in management (Jones, 1992), assessment and teaching (Steel, 1991), and curriculum development and review (Tilstone, 1991). Such exhortation is a launching pad for support services who are required to work in a collaborative manner. Thomas states:

> a decade of experience has shown us what we should have appreciated at the outset: groups and teams are fragile, fickle creatures. Bringing people together to work on a project – especially if they aren't prepared for it – can do more harm than good. To work well they need a lot of help.

> (Thomas, 1992, p.197)

Help should come in the form of joint training which is aimed at developing collaborative working skills.

Curriculum and assessment

Support services have developed to give pupils with diverse needs access to the mainstream curriculum. Ongoing assessment examines whether this access is being achieved. The reasons for support services to exist are to:

- make staff aware of children with difficulties in learning;
- develop the skills of the classroom staff;

- prepare differentiated materials for pupil use;
- provide specialist information;
- carry out in-service training;
- consult and advise staff;
- support with whole school initiatives;
- work directly with the pupils and assess their changing needs;
- ensure a curriculum for *all*.

Historically support staff have worked in comparative isolation concentrating upon certain areas of the curriculum. With the advent of the National Curriculum we see opportunities for support staff to become more involved with *whole* school policies, *whole* staff meetings and *whole* curriculum developments for the benefit of the *whole* child. In Chapters 4 and 5 there will be in-depth discussions centring upon these issues with suggested strategies for their implementation.

Currently support personnel are questioning whether there is 'any light at the end of the Education Reform Act tunnel'? This chapter has covered some factors which we think can be considered as 'starting blocks' in the continuous development of support services. It has suggested that recent legislation such as The Education Reform Act, The Children Act and the Elton Report provide the opportunity for support services to collaborate. Such collaboration can enhance the skills of all who are working with children with diverse needs. Before such collaboration can be implemented services should:

1. undertake an internal audit;
2. develop service agreements;
3. design contracts.

In addition to:

- developing marketing strategies and
- linking in with Local Authority developments.

These are considered essential to the evolution of services and their preparation for survival in a 'market-led' education system.

Part II

Curriculum and Assessment

CHAPTER 4

Whole Child, Whole Curriculum

In this chapter we shall examine in detail the current trends in the curriculum in mainstream and special schools. We shall be discussing ways in which specialist support staff can work at the centre of this curriculum rather than on the periphery as they often do now. The view of a unified curriculum will be presented and its potential for enhancing collaborative work between professionals will be explored.

Perspectives on the current curriculum

The advent of the National Curriculum has managed to bring together the respective curricula of mainstream and special classrooms. Although it is an overstatement to claim that we truly have 'a curriculum for all' as promised in Curriculum Guidance 2 (NCC, 1989), many of the differences that have kept special education apart from the mainstream can be seen more as variations in an eclectic view of meeting the individual needs of pupils. However, in order to understand the present position more fully, it is necessary to separate out the two strands of development. We shall begin by looking at influences on curriculum in special education (whether it takes place in special or ordinary schools).

Curriculum for special needs

There can be no doubt that the influence of educational psychology on special education has been enormous. In fact, it could be said, they grew up together. The struggle for scientific respectability of educational psychology has had much influence on our thinking and this has had the effect of placing this branch of education firmly in a scientific-medical stratum. This interrelationship can be appreciated by studying the origins of behavioural teaching, psychoanalysis, psychometric testing and cognitive development theory.

Acknowledging this close relationship goes some way towards understanding how both curriculum and teaching methods have evolved in special education. It certainly explains the development of programmes such as SNAP (Special Needs Action Programme) (Ainscow and Muncey, 1981), Portage (Bluma *et al.*, 1976) and EDY (Education of the Developmentally Young) (McBrien and Foxen, 1981). All these programmes, and many others, have a theoretical base in behavioural psychology with its emphasis on structured situations for learning to master highly specific tasks. Small steps to success are carefully written by the teacher and taken by pupils at their own pace. Rewards are available often in many guises from successfully completing a task to teacher praise or tangibles such as stars or food.

Although many pupils for whom learning is difficult have gained enormously from this concentration upon the minutiae of specific tasks, it has had the effect of narrowing the curriculum offered to them. Difficulties in reading or mathematics has tended to mean extra reading and mathematics for these pupils to the exclusion of other more enriching experiences. Children with severe learning difficulties have often been restricted to a complete diet of social training as these are seen as the most important basic skills for learning to live independent lives as adults. Attention to wider experiences has not been evident, or certainly has not been given credence in the pressure to demonstrate the learning of skills.

The criticisms of writers such as McConkey (1981) in the world of severe learning difficulties and Ainscow and Tweddle (1988) in special needs in mainstream education, have challenged special educators to re-examine the curriculum offered in schools. No longer is there such a strong influence from behavioural psychology, this has been tempered by an interest in a social interactionist view of children learning through their own active engagement with adults and the environment. Developing understanding and problem solving are given a more prominent place and the curriculum is no longer seen in terms of a division into 'core' skills and 'extended' experiences, but as more of a whole, meeting the diverse needs of individual pupils. The wider curriculum can be seen to become the means through which key knowledge, skills, understanding and attitudes can develop.

A curriculum for all

Although the National Curriculum had been heralded by its writers as a curriculum for all pupils, there was very little to encourage teachers of pupils with special needs as it was introduced. At first, these needs were completely ignored and then a complicated system of modifications and disapplications was devised which appeared to exclude rather than include pupils whose needs are not straight-forward. Other parts of the 1988 Education Act offer related problems with the emphasis on standards and competition between schools and authorities. Wedell (1988) drew our attention to possible difficulties when the Education Bill was first introduced. He raised doubts that the government's purpose, to provide:

> A better education – relevant to the late twentieth century and beyond – for all our children whatever their ability, wherever they live, whatever type of school their parents choose for them.
>
> (DES, 1987a)

could be fulfilled through the proposals that schools should compete through examination results. Certainly, producing a National Curriculum for everyone does not guarantee that what will be delivered will be right for every pupil and his or her needs.

The group of educationalists for whom the advent of the National Curriculum has been the greatest challenge, is that responsible for the teaching and learning of pupils with the most severe and complex difficulties. Faced with the possibility of being marginalised or even excluded wholesale from the new initiative, teachers in this branch of education, galvanised themselves into action. Some of the curriculum material that has been produced in the name of providing access for pupils with severe and complex learning needs has challenged both the traditional curriculum for special needs and the new National Curriculum (Fagg *et al.*, 1990; NCC, 1992). There have been critics who have pointed to the possibility of tokenism if we suggest that we are studying science when we are teaching toilet training (Staff of Tye Green School, 1991), but on the whole, the response of the majority of teachers has been positive as can be seen from the work of groups such as the West Midlands National Curriculum Monitoring Group (SLD), the North West National Curriculum Group and the Special Educational Needs Resources Centre in the North East.

There has been great enthusiasm engendered for widening the

curriculum to include science, technology, history and geography, subjects rarely seen in special schools in the early 1980s. Many teachers found that they were in fact already teaching many aspects of the new orders issued for the National Curriculum, but under different names. Some teachers did react by declaring that they had spent years developing a curriculum that was right for their pupils and they did not want to be forced into changing to something which did not meet their needs (Emblem and Conti-Ramsden, 1990; Ware, 1990). This dilemma is still not resolved and teachers are far from feeling that the National Curriculum is the answer to all curriculum needs in special education.

There are, however, many aspects of both the statutory and non-statutory orders for the new curriculum which have been, or will be, of considerable benefit to curriculum development in special education. Not the least of these is the feeling that educational need can be seen on a continuum applicable to all individuals, even those with the most severe difficulties. Even though many of these pupils may be unlikely to progress very far through the prescribed levels, the feeling that they can be seen as working *within* Level 1 contributes to this ideal of a continuum (NCC, 1992). There is far less of a feeling of separateness which although it does not guarantee a significant move away from segregation towards integration, the seeds are sown for this to happen in the future.

It would be foolish to suggest that this view is prevalent throughout the educational world. There are far too many factors working against the ideal of a continuum of individual needs for the National Curriculum to solve. Years of vested interest in a separate special education system in both mainstream and special schools creates a world that will be difficult to dismantle. It is certainly hard to see, in the present astringent climate, how schools could begin to meet all the diverse needs of a full range of pupils without an enormous reshuffling of resources.

The demands on schools to raise standards through competition is of little help either. It merely contributes to the feeling that the more challenging of individual needs are too costly in time and effort for them to attempt to meet them. If standards are to be the driving force influencing resources then those schools with a preponderance of difficult individual needs will find it hard to compete. Integration links with special schools will not be seen as important, in fact they may even be seen as unwelcome distractions from the business of 'raising standards'. There is already a worrying trend reported by teachers in the West Midlands towards limiting integration projects which will make it difficult for the ideal of the continuum of need to be realised in the near future.

It is very easy to become depressed and feel that curricular initiatives can have very little effect on the years of history. That is not the impression we wish to convey in this chapter in our efforts to counteract accusations of unrealistic idealism. There is certainly much to encourage all who work within special education if the statutory demands are accompanied by imaginative teaching which draws on work developed through classroom experience and research. There is a growing body of teachers who are beginning to share their classroom work in order that others may benefit from the experience. There has long been a call for easier dissemination of research findings, particularly from serving teachers, and, if you are prepared to search, this can now be found (Wedell, 1985). The publications of the Manchester Fellows (Fagg *et al.,* 1990) and the Cambridge National Curriculum Team (NCC, 1992; Lawson, 1992; Rose, 1991) are well founded in classroom work and although both are aimed specifically at pupils with severe learning difficulties, the suggestions are applicable in much wider contexts.

We have a particular interest in the suggestions made by Byers, one of the teachers involved in the Cambridge team, concerning the development of 'integrated schemes of work' (Byers, 1990) as the next part of this chapter will focus on how we can make the curriculum, of which the National Curriculum is part, work for pupils with a variety of different needs and a variety of different 'teachers'. The whole question of how we present the different parts of the whole using the many different professionals found in schools without giving the child a fragmented view will dominate the next pages.

Unifying the curriculum

The subject bias of the National Curriculum has heightened the awareness of many teachers for the need to improve the manner in which pupils are encouraged to view the curriculum as a whole. Traditionally in the primary school, unification of some subjects has been achieved by working through a thematic or project approach. This has been often confined to history and geography with aspects of other subjects contributing on occasions. In the secondary school, thematic approaches are often difficult to find at all unless pupils are working under the mantle of Technical and Vocational Education (TVE).

HMI have been particularly critical of the topic work they have observed in the primary school (DES, 1978a; 1989b; 1990a). They found much of it was badly planned and led to inconsequential or even continually repeated learning which contributed little to pupils' understanding of how the parts of the curriculum came together as a whole. There have been useful attempts to counteract these criticisms which, although many date from pre National Curriculum days, can offer much to teachers as they struggle to fit topic work into the new order.

Before we turn to the practicalities of effective cross curricular work in classrooms and the way in which specialist staff can contribute, it will be helpful to consider why we should want to unify the curriculum. What are the arguments for presenting learning in this manner and why is it so difficult to achieve in the present educational climate

It has often been said that children, especially young children, do not divide their learning up into small pieces as is traditional with a subject-based approach to the curriculum or an approach which differentiates between 'basic skills' and 'the extended curriculum'. Defining and specifying these skills is very difficult and doing so can actually be counter-productive because of the simplistic utilitarian view of education that it produces (Blenkin and Kelly, 1981). The message from the government, in the 1990s, supports this utilitarian view so it is very difficult for teachers to explore the alternatives suggested by those who support a process-orientated rather than product-orientated curriculum.

An over-dependence upon end-products can lead teachers and learners to become core curriculum-driven with basic skills being afforded an over-inflated place of importance. There have been many powerful advocates of 'traditional' subjects and training in 'basic skills', from the Black Papers of the 1970s (Cox and Boyson, 1975) to recent Secretaries of State for Education. Critics suggest that such people are looking back to a golden age of education which has not really ever existed. Certainly, the present thinking behind the National Curriculum seems to dismiss or at least ignore the wealth of curriculum research carried out in the last twenty years. Child-centred education, championed by The Plowden Report (DES, 1967), has been branded as woolly, progressive nonsense and teachers are being bullied into retracing their steps to the time when only the few academic high-fliers succeeded at the expense of all the rest. The Alexander Report (DES, 1992) has been frequently quoted to support this view, although careful reading reveals a much less damning evaluation of primary education than the press would have us believe.

A common curriculum

The three HMI Red Books published between 1977 and 1983 advocate a common curriculum rather than a national curriculum. There is considerable support within these documents for teaching and learning to cross traditional subject barriers in a genuine attempt to meet individual needs. There is a focus on the quality of the teaching rather than on the bureaucratic ways in which outcomes can be measured and compared, as can be found in the National Curriculum.

The manner in which HMI viewed the curriculum is demonstrated in their checklist of eight areas of experience:

- the aesthetic and creative
- the ethical
- the linguistic
- the mathematical
- the physical
- the scientific
- the social and political
- the spiritual

(DES,1977, p.6)

Although they do indicate how this would translate into subjects in the secondary school, the authors of the Red Book add:

> it is not proposed that schools should plan and construct a common curriculum in terms of subject labels only: that would be to risk becoming trapped in discussions about the relative importance of this subject or that. Rather it is necessary to look through the subject or discipline to the areas of experience and knowledge to which it may provide access, and to the skills and attitudes which it might assist to develop.
>
> (DES,1977, p.6)

It will be difficult to fulfil this advice through the core and foundation subjects of the National Curriculum as enshrined in the

1988 Education Act. Teachers will have to be very determined to cross subject barriers and demonstrate how learning is inter-related if the vision of HMI is to be realised.

Cross curricular elements

Some cross-curricular aspects of the core and foundation subjects are included in the document *The Whole Curriculum* (NCC, 1990) and although there may be considerable criticism of the Tory-orientated subject matter of the suggested themes, there is much that is of use to teachers in mainstream and special schools. Ashdown *et al.* (1991) suggest that the skills, dimension and themes 'should form the bedrock upon which to set the core and foundation subjects' (p.14), particularly for pupils with special needs. The emphasis on work experience, the building of self esteem, all aspects of health education and learning to become independent citizens have for many years been central to the curriculum in the secondary departments of special schools. In the cross curricular elements of the National Curriculum these have become recognised and given status. If teachers really address these issues in their curriculum delivery the most restricting aspects of subject teaching can be counteracted.

Topic work

Despite its bad press in the 1990s, topic work has much to offer as a curricular organisational tool, especially in the crowded curriculum we have today. In the discussion which follows, we will concentrate on primary schools and departments but hasten to add that many parts of the secondary curriculum can and are taught in a manner related closely to topic work.

> Topic work includes all those areas of the curriculum (other than basic reading and number skills) which are explored in a thematic way. Topics may be (predominately) scientific, mathematical, or in the field of humanities; or they may be interdisciplinary.
>
> (Kerry and Eggleston, 1988, p.18)

This definition came out of a research study carried out by Kerry and Eggleston and is a useful starting point for understanding how best to carry out this work. To this we must add the need for precise and specific planning if pupils are to gain the most from the provision of a context to practise basic skills. Many schools decide on topics for study, terms or even years in advance in order that learning can be characterised by progression rather than being haphazard. The approach, for example in Coventry primary schools in the 1980s was to plan for the whole seven years of primary schooling. One of the planning tools was the matrix illustrated in Fig 4.1, which enabled teachers to identify key concepts and ideas allied to key content categories. In this way, there was a greater likelihood of maintaining a balance in the curriculum whilst achieving more breadth and depth in the humanities and sciences.

Figure 4.1   Key Concepts and Key Content Categories

Key
Concepts   Key Content Categories

	another culture	man-made system	human community	non human community	natural system
adaptation					
energy					
protection					
conquest					
migration					

A key concept and a key idea allied to a key content category will produce a topic title. For example:

KEY CONCEPT	Adaptation
KEY CONTENT CATEGORY	Natural system
KEY IDEA(S)	1. Living things adapt to their environment
	2. There are consequences for unsuccessful attempts at adaptation
TOPIC TITLE	The Development of Life on Earth before Man
	(Coventry LEA, 1987)

Part of the planning for topic work has been provided through the Statutory Orders for the National Curriculum. The content has now been stipulated, although the means by which we teach this content is still in our hands. School and classroom organisation skills are much needed if topic work is to be delivered in a way which counteracts the criticisms often expressed concerning lack of cohesion and superficial learning. This is especially important for pupils whose learning needs are difficult to meet.

Tann's (1988) study revealed very varied approaches to topic work from forty different teachers. These are represented in Fig. 4.2.

Figure 4.2   Characteristics of Integrated Curriculum Practice

Control	teacher directed	teacher and children negotiate	children unaided or children evolve group/class study
Content focus	single/combined subject	multi-disciplinary	main interest followed
Context	whole class doing similar work	groups doing related work	individuals on own projects
Place in the curriculum	'basic' in morning, 'other' in afternoon		fully integrated day
Resources	secondary sources (book-based)	audio-visual e.g.: watch programme/talks	primary sources, first-hand experience and experiments
Audience	for teacher to assess	for class to share	for others to respond to e.g.: parents, community
Records	none list of titles	outlines of webs kept centrally	logs kept by child, parent, teacher – comments and evaluation

(Tann, 1988, p.23)

Plotting different approaches along a continuum is a very useful tool for teachers as they plan for the children's learning. For instance, if we consider the *context* continuum, if pupils only experience working as individuals on their own 'project', they will develop good skills in the area of working independently but will not have the opportunity to develop social skills through working in a group. Teachers need to plan to include possibilities along the whole continuum and not feel that topics are always run in the same way.

Planning topic work can no longer be satisfied by the large sheet of paper containing the topic 'web' of the disparate ideas pulled together under the guise of offering breadth of interest. This might be a starting point but in order to ensure coverage of and progression through the curriculum, it will be necessary to plan well ahead and decide precisely what each topic will contain. If there is some flexibility then there can also be times set aside for pupils to pursue interests of their own, so that the *control* is not always in the hands of the teacher. Good plans contain a mixture of 'things that must be covered' and 'things that could be covered'. Evaluation of the topic at the end should reveal some surprises which fit into neither and indicate the teacher's ability to respond to individual pupil's needs and interests.

The example in Fig 4.3 from a primary school illustrates the ways in which one teacher planned and carried out part of a topic in her classroom as part of a whole school approach to cross curricular work.

The recording of evidence of learning from topic work can present teachers with considerable difficulties. Every child cannot be watched all the time and teachers do not have the time to make copious notes on every learning step. One way to solve the problem is to devise ways in which pupils can complete their own records. Involving pupils in their own recording in this way can offer extremely useful learning opportunities. Involvement can begin at the planning stage as group or individual record sheets are drawn up according to particular need. Agreement can be reached over the evidence of learning that will be produced and how it will be presented and stored.

Time will need to be set aside for the more formal aspects of assessment but again these can involve pupils fully. The following example observed in a primary school illustrates how one teacher managed this.

Figure 4.3   Record Sheets

Subject/ Attainment Targets	Assessment	Cross Curricular Dimensions & Skills	Activity/Task Paying Attention to Extension and Repetition Work	Organisation Indicate role of S.S	Resources/ Equipment	Time in Hours (Est.)
			Key Ideas People can talk to each other from a long way away. *Introduction* Watch TV Programme Stop, Look & Listen (1) 'Postman' 490			
Science AT2, 1a 2a Eng AT1	Eng AT1 2a	Communication	*Topic Day Activities* (1) Make a short video recording of members of the group talking about selves etc. Play to other groups later.	3 mixed-ability group takes turns at all 3 activities S.S with group.	Stop, Look & Listen cass (1) Video camera & tape	30 mins
			(2) Take the children to visit Sec's Office to see telephones type-writer etc. (Get permission first)	Teacher with group		1 hr 30 mins total
		Creative	(3) Children design the picture side of a postcard, draw and colour.	Self-directed.	Card cut into postcard size.	
English AT3		Creative Communication	*Other Activities* (1) Choose some of the postcards above, write address and send to people in school. Take some children to post them.	Teacher with groups. Sec 11.	Postcards above, stamps (or buy stamps from PO).	45 mins
		Study	(2) Ask the children to find out their telephone numbers. Make a class telephone directory, having looked at a real one.			

Subject/ Attainment Targets	Assessment	Cross Curricular Dimensions & Skills	Activity/Task Paying Attention to Extension and Repetition Work	Organisation Inidicate role of S.S	Resources/ Equipment	Time in Hours (Est.)
Eng AT4 Level 2d Maths AT2			Yr 2 children help to put names into alphabetical order (as appropriate).	Teacher with Yr 2s	Book for directory	1 hr
			Yr 1 children write numbers on telephone dial and push-button on w/sheet.	Self-directed	w/sheet	
Eng AT1			(3) Make tape-recordings eg the class singing or saying a poem, individual children telling jokes etc. Red/yellow classes swap and listen.	Teacher with class or groups	Tape recorder Blank tape	odd times total
		Creative practical	(4) Make a mini class newspaper on one large sheet of paper. Children contribute written news, pictures, puzzles as appropriate.	Teacher and EA, with groups and class as appropriate.	Paper glue and children's work.	30 mins 15 mins
History AT1, 2c		Imaginative	(5) Talk about the days when there were no TV, telephones, radio etc. How did people talk to each other from a long way away? Talk about early postal system, bad roads, delays etc. Verbal messages as many people couldn't write.	Teacher with class.	Folio on computer	10 mins

Subject/ Attainment Targets	Assessment	Cross Curricular Dimensions & Skills	Activity/Task Paying Attention to Extension and Repetition Work	Organisation Inidicate role of S.S	Resources/ Equipment	Time in Hours (Est.)
			Send some children with messages to remember and say to other staff members. Did they remember?			15 mins
Geog AT4 2c		Study	(6) Look at world map. Identify countries where children have visited or have relations. Talk about how we can talk to them.	Teacher with class.	world map	10 mins
Science AT12	Sc AT12/2a		Children complete w/sheet as appropriate (mostly Yr 2s). Yr 1s draw themselves talking to someone on telephone — they choose someone special or unusual.	Individual	w/sheet	30 mins
Art/craft		Creative	(7) Children continue work or frieze.	Teacher & S.S with groups.	Collage materials as appropriate.	1 hr
Technology			(8) Children continue project on playground (see technology planning).	D.H. with Yr groups	As planned	1 hr
			(9) TV Thinkabout Cassette 2 'Signals' 884 – Thinkabout – 'Getting the Message'	Teacher with class	Thinkabout Cassette 2	30 mins

Example (mainstream primary school)

Mrs Harris took aside eight infant pupils to help them fill in part of their record sheets for their topic called 'Finding our way about'. They had been working on maps and their local area. The record sheet contained 'I can do' statements such as 'I can talk about maps' . The group talked for some time and then were helped to fill in an appropriate statement. One six year old wrote 'I can talk about co-ordinates' and another asked the teacher to write that she could find her own street on the map of the local area. There was space for Mrs Harris to record a quick evaluation of each child's performance in the form of a triangle. One side drawn meant 'skill practised', two sides drawn meant 'some improvement' and all three sides drawn meant 'very good progress'. The children were consulted over how much of the triangle should be drawn and no disagreements were witnessed!

Perhaps it needs to be added that while Mrs Harris was working with a small group of eight pupils, the rest of the class were engaged in independent activities. Many were working together in pairs or small groups helping each other so that the assessment was not interrupted. Much planning had gone into this and pupils were well experienced in being resourceful before resorting to requesting help from the teacher. They were co-managers with the teacher in the classroom.

At first glance, it may be suggested that pupils with more severe learning difficulties could not manage to be involved in their own curriculum planning and recording. The beginnings of such an approach can be seen in the basic offering of choice even with pupils who might be defined as having profound and multiple learning difficulties. A simple switch device can help youngsters to control what is happening around them thus helping them through the first step of curricular choice. Providing photographs and artefacts can help with recall of activities which can contribute towards negotiated record keeping. In these circumstances, the teacher becomes an advocate for the pupils, providing a framework for everyone to be appropriately involved in their own learning.

The next case study is taken from a school for pupils with severe learning difficulties and illustrates how a topic can be used to embrace all the different needs of the pupils within a class group. Pupil involvement is at the centre of the approach.

Example (Special School – Secondary Department)
A group of eight teenagers were involved in a topic on 'clothes'. Six of them were working on basic literacy skills and also needed a chance for some work experience. Two of them had more profound learning difficulties and their needs could be best met through work involving basic communication skills. All pupils were involved in the topic but each had an individual programme tailored to meet their own needs.

Amongst other activities, the six more able young people set out to run a school laundry service. As the school catered for pupils from 2–19 with many who were incontinent, there was plenty of opportunity for washing, drying and sorting clothes. The following timetable demonstrates how they ran the service and indicates the skills, knowledge and understanding involved in the project.

> Sign in for work
> Put on overalls
> Collect clipboard of list of charges
> Collect clothes from each class
> Record number/type of items on clipboard
> Sort washing according to care needed (reading labels)
> Use washing machine
> Estimate time of return
> Work out charges and make out bills for each class
> Hang out washing or put it in drier
> Estimate time of return (probably lunch time)
> Take in washing or remove from drier
> Fold clothes/match socks/sort into piles
> Iron anything appropriate
> Match clothes to clipboard list to sort into classes
> Return correct clothes to correct class
> Charge correct money and give change
> Count all money taken
> 'Bank' money with school secretary
> Check all is put away and tidy
> Take off overall
> Sign out

The money was recyclable and was given out to each class by the secretary at the beginning of each day of the work experience. Real money was earned for the service and used to buy ingredients for sandwiches for lunch. This was money that was already allocated to the group, but at this time the emphasis was on earning it rather than it just appearing.

To begin with the whole cycle took more than one day. Clothes washed one day were returned the next but later in the project, the work force speeded up and managed to complete the work load in one day.

The two pupils with PMLD spent some of their time with the group and the rest on physiotherapy exercises, sensory work and pre-verbal communication. Their time with the main group centred around experiencing the interaction possible with more able peers.

The individual needs of each pupil were subsumed within the overall project. For example, John was working in the following areas:

Writing his full name

Reading within a social context

Simple addition and subtraction to 20

Giving change using all coins (help needed over £1)

Setting a timer using minutes

Safety in using electricity

Co-operative work within a small group

Problem solving in natural contexts

Mary had different priorities:

Recognising her first name

Matching objects according to colour/size

Recognising simple symbols (Makaton)

Remembering and delivering simple messages (three word level)

Finding her way round school

Working with a partner for a few minutes

Fine motor skills using pincer grip

Both pupils were able to work within the project and staff were able to differentiate the curriculum sufficiently to encompass the diversity of need found in the group.

There is no reason why the traditional topics associated with primary schools should not be able to encompass pupils' individual objectives in the way demonstrated in this work experience topic. Byers (1990) writes of work on, what he calls 'integrated schemes of work', carried out in special schools in the Local Education

Authorities in the DES Eastern Region. He explains that this is a combination of traditional topic work and objectives-based teaching which enables the best of both methods to be employed in ensuring continuity and progression tailored to individual needs. He suggests that this is a valuable format for helping teachers in schools for pupils with severe learning difficulties to teach in a cross curricular manner without losing educational rigour.

Working in this manner has a much wider use than just in schools for pupils with SLDs. If true diversity of learning need is to be met in any school, then this combination of precision and cross curricular experience deserves to be considered. It would certainly counter the criticisms of poor progression and continuity pinpointed at the beginning of this section. It would ensure that teachers would be able to employ more planning tools than just the ubiquitous topic web.

Putting the periphery into the core

It has been argued in this chapter that children and young people learn best when their work is presented in a cross curricular manner and is not fragmented into small chunks taught out of context. This is not to deny that there are times when skills and concepts need to be highlighted when they do not necessarily fit into the latest topic. It can become very contrived if all activities *have* to be included.

There are, however, many times when staff from the various support services could plan for their priorities for individual pupils to correspond much more closely with the cross curricular themes found in the classroom. Many mainstream schools have moved on from the old style remedial department withdrawal methods towards learning support in the classroom (see Chapter 1). It is not unusual to find more than one professional working together in the same room. However, working side-by-side does not necessarily guarantee a collaborative view of the curriculum and the learning needs of all pupils.

Example (mainstream primary school)
Mrs Frank is employed by a primary school as a learning support teacher. She works with groups of children and individual pupils. Sometimes she works with the most able groups so that the class teacher can concentrate on the rest of the class. She is skilled at adapting worksheets to suit the

diversity of abilities presented by the pupils. She is also on hand to explain practical activities where necessary.

Her own criticism of the system centres on the fact that she is not included in many of the planning meetings. Often she is *told* about topics and activities and is expected to adapt the work for the individuals and groups that she supports. It is very difficult for her to feel part of the staff teams in these circumstances.

It is certainly not easy to attend every planning meeting when you support several different teams in the school, but here there seems to be a serious lack of any co-ordination. The result is frustration on the part of the teacher as she is constantly teaching other people's ideas rather than her own, and a threat to continuity and progression for the pupils as she does not always know what has preceded the current work.

A diagrammatic representation of this fragmented curriculum can be seen in Fig. 4.4.

This is contrasted with a more collaborative view.

In order for true collaboration to take place, it is necessary for members of the support services to meet regularly with classroom staff. Not all members can meet weekly all together. This is an unrealistic ideal. The next example is taken from a school for pupils with physical disabilities and it illustrates the way one set of professionals have managed the collaboration procedure to enable the delivery of a unified, inter-disciplinary curriculum.

Example (special school for pupils with physical disabilities)
At least once a year, in preparation for the annual review, all the members of the multi-disciplinary team meet and discuss each individual pupil. This is organised by the class teacher with help from the teacher who holds the post of responsibility for multi-disciplinary work. At this meeting the different professionals involved review the work in the previous year and discuss priorities for the year ahead. Although they have different priorities according to their discipline or specialism, they work together to be able to offer a cohesive package to address the needs of the child under review.

After this initial meeting, different members of the team consult with and work with each other at different times. The occupational therapist and physiotherapist were observed

Figure 4.4a   Fragmented Curriculum

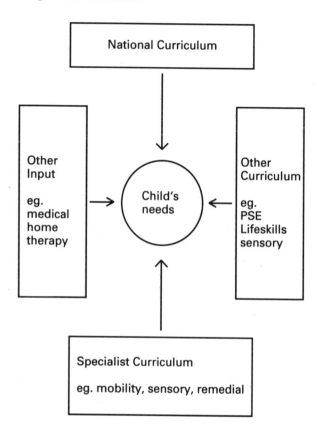

working together with a child to find a suitable mode of communication for her. They had to consider her seating position, her hand function, her motor control and her intellectual ability. Before this session, the occupational therapist had been in consultation with the teacher, to help her select the correct programme to use on the computer in order that the child could be working within her normal curriculum whilst they found the correct switch for her to use.

Although professionals working together can be found in many settings, it is quite rare for the curriculum to be considered, especially when the professionals are from a paramedical background. In this particular school, much work has gone into building up the kind of collaboration which includes all angles of the pupil. The physiotherapist works vocabulary from the latest curriculum

Figure 4.4b   Collaborative Curriculum

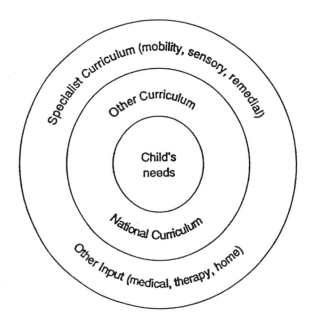

topic into exercise sessions; seating position is considered extremely important in lessons where no therapist is present; mobility is encouraged around the school within and between lessons and everyone tries to keep to the speech therapist's priorities when they talk to the children.

There is little doubt that in these circumstances, pupils are receiving a more unified and inter-disciplinary curriculum than they would be if the professionals concentrated exclusively on their own area of work. There is also little doubt that working together in this way involves more work. Individuals must be prepared to meet together and exchange ideas, listen to each other's priorities and incorporate them in their own work. In many ways this is easier to achieve when the professionals share a discipline (such as a class teacher and a specialist teacher of the visually impaired) than when they come from different backgrounds.

Ways of creating and working in effective teams will feature in the next chapter, but before we turn to this aspect, we will address some of the practicalities of creating a unified and collaborative curriculum.

Work through a topic

At this point we will return to cross curricular work and suggest useful stages through which professionals can go in order to develop programmes of study for individual and groups of pupils in their care using a thematic approach. The various specialisms and disciplines can be involved for as much or as little time as the pupils' needs dictate. The examples offered are taken from a variety of mainstream and special school settings but they all revolve around the same theme and could be adapted to almost any situation.

Figure 4.5   Topic Web (mainstream primary or special school)

PE
popmobility
folk dancing
sports
special olympics
(physiotherapy)

SCIENCE
heart rate
body as a
machine
body needs
diet
using muscles
(sensory
specialists)

TECHNOLOGY
cooking healthy
diet
design charts for
exercise

MATHEMATICS
counting
exercises
exercise charts
timing sports
pulse rates

KEEPING FIT

LITERACY
list of exercises
work out charts
football results
leaflets on health

GEOGRAPHY
orienteering
pitch layouts
location of
football
teams on map
(mobility)

THE ARTS
design a t-shirt
posters for
games
popmobility
music
football songs
folk dancing

**SPEAKING &
LISTENING**
body vocabulary
radio
commentary
pep talks
(speech therapy)

HISTORY
past scores &
records
olympics
movement
games in history

SELF HELP
showering &
dressing
looking after the
body
(occupational
therapy)

Keeping fit

Stage 1

Brainstorm ideas for a topic web including different activities at all levels of ability. If peripatetic staff cannot be present at this initial meeting, then teachers should remember to give due consideration to the specialist and medical needs of pupils, ready for more detailed consultation at stage 3.

Stage 2

Relate these ideas to the whole curriculum of which the National Curriculum is part. Many special schools will have a highly developed curriculum alongside the National Curriculum which will influence the eventual path of the topic. Some topics can be all embracing and develop over several weeks, others are much smaller in scope and cannot encompass all areas of the curriculum.

Stage 3

Consult with the specialist staff who work with the pupils so that everyone has a chance to contribute to the on-going work. If everyone is aware of the topic in hand and the proposed activities then there is a greater likelihood of the child being regarded as a whole person for whom a whole curriculum can be devised.

Examples (a. special school)
Mr S. (class teacher) discussed the needs of three of his pupils who worked with the physiotherapist on a regular basis. Between them they devised a set of popmobility exercises that would benefit each pupil and agreed that work on how the body works would be emphasised by both teacher and physio. The devised exercises would become the set for the whole class with some extensions for those more physically able. They also arranged that the physio would become more specifically involved in the preparation for a fun sports day at the end of the topic.
(b.) mainstream school)
Mrs B. has 2 pupils in her class who are partially sighted. As

usual she discussed lighting and size of print for topic work with the specialist teacher of the visually impaired. They also considered a specialist input into the orienteering part of the topic, combining both geographical and mobility angles. The VI specialist put aside some time in the second half of the term to offer extra help for this.

Stage 4

Plan group and individual schemes of work to meet all aspects of the children's needs. Some activities will need very careful planning to enable pupils to demonstrate evidence of learning. Not all parts of the topic will need to be treated in the same exact manner. Some activities will be offered mainly for experience or as a context for practising a skill which has already been divided into small steps.

Example (special school − secondary department)
Group activity − cooking a healthy diet

SESSION 1
Discuss suitable lunch to cook, remembering work done concerning balanced diet. Consult cookery books/cards and make a shopping list of ingredients for cooking.

Individual objectives
John will use the concept keyboard to make a personal shopping list containing things he is allowed for his healthy diet (coeliac)
   Mary will act as scribe for the group shopping list, using 'look, cover and write' as a technique.

SESSION 2
Do the shopping at the supermarket. Different pupils or groups of pupils can be responsible for separate items or transactions.

Individual objectives
Elizabeth will give the correct money for her item from a selection of coins in her purse.

Mark will select the correct amount of unbruised fruit for everyone in his group.

SESSION 3
Prepare the lunch and eat it. This could be organised like a production line or one group can be the cooks at a time with a chance for others in the following weeks.

Individual objectives
Peter will demonstrate a basic knowledge of hygiene in the kitchen, including hand washing. He will contribute to a verbal list of do's and don'ts as the group works.

Alim will divide food into half or two equal portions on request.

(Although these have been written as individual objectives they could easily be appropriate for several pupils at a similar stage.)

Stage 5

Assessment possibilities need to be planned so that evidence of learning is considered before the activities take place. Pupil self recording should be built in and there should be opportunities for unusual events to be recognised. Assessment by specialist staff also needs consideration as does the mechanism for sharing any information gathered. (See Chapter 5 for more detail on assessment.)

Example (secondary special school)
Robert will be working on using various means of timing in relation to keeping fit. He will experiment with a sand timer but will eventually use a stop watch. He can already tell the time on a digital watch and understands the scale of measurement from minutes to hours, although any estimation of time is rather hazy and he needs practice in using and interpreting the stop watch. Seconds will be introduced and related to his own digital watch as well as the stop watch. In order for his teacher to assess progress made in this area, Robert will need to have plenty of opportunities for estimating and timing races of various kinds. Some will happen in the classroom and can involve timing cars rolling down a slope or classmates writing

out their multiplication tables etc. Other opportunities need to be given out on the field or in the hall and more specifically part of the topic in hand. Written work will need to include simple comparison of times to decide winners and losers. (Calculations will not include any conversion of seconds to minutes.)

Robert will be encouraged to be involved in the record keeping by completing a simple diary of what he has done and setting himself a goal for the next session. A summary sheet will be filled in at the end of the time spent on the topic. It will contain the following statements:

> I can time a runner or someone doing exercises using a stop watch
>
> I can write down the time from the stop watch
>
> I can tell who is the fastest and slowest of four competitors

There will be space for other statements not pre-decided.

Stage 6

Only at stage 6 is the topic ready for the classroom. Pupils will be working on the planned activities in small and large groups as well as individuals so, at this stage, classroom management aspects become very important. Collaborative teaching will often be appropriate as specialist support staff move in and out of the work in hand.

Example (mainstream primary school)
Mr T. (class teacher) and Ms K. (learning support teacher) are working together with a class of primary aged pupils on the writing and reading aspects of the topic. Their planning has included a rich diversity of activities to suit all abilities in the class. The range is very wide (National Curriculum level 1–4) and they both work at all levels.

Mr T. has a group of six pupils and they are working together to devise an information leaflet on the relationship between exercise and a healthy heart. After checking they are all able to contribute, he leaves them and joins a group who are working individually on writing out their own exercise routines worked out in the last PE session. He checks that John is forming the letters o, a, c, d, g in the correct orientation and that Saleem is using the aids offered round the room when he needs to copy words. He records some observations about the group in his notebook and moves on...

Ms K., in the meantime, has been conducting a mixed ability group reading session using a story that fits into the topic. The emphasis has been on comprehension and then on inventing their own ending to fit the beginning. She records short sentences about each of the eight members of the group. The session finishes with a brief review of what they did and what they felt they had learned.

This is only a snapshot of this classroom and some of the work in this particular session. The two teachers, working together are able to meet the needs of pupils with a very wide range of ability. They use their planning time wisely, so that they can work towards the same objectives and record progress in the same way. They exchange observations and notes (where something out of the ordinary has happened) at the end of the session.

Stage 7

After the planning, implementation and assessment phases comes the evaluative stage when staff and pupils look back on the work achieved. These may, or may not, be formal meetings. Sometimes very valuable evaluation happens in the classroom, over lunch or in the corridor. Teachers are looking for feedback on the enjoyment of all concerned and the value of the topic chosen as a vehicle for well-motivated effective learning, meeting the needs of all pupils involved. Mechanisms for collaborative work between staff also need evaluation to aid further development.

Example (special school)
Mrs P. (class teacher) met Mrs L. (speech therapist) over lunch to discuss how well the topic had worked from her angle. All ten pupils in the class had speech and language therapy input of some kind and Mrs L. had worked within the topic on one morning a week between break and dinner time, keeping her eye on the needs of everyone.

During the evaluation, Mrs L. went through her records of each pupil, and they discussed any progress as she went. Mrs P. took a few notes to add to the pupils' individual records. They finished the thirty minute session with a brief outline of the speech and language priorities for the next topic. They agreed another meeting time to discuss a proposed language recording sheet. This would need to be a much bigger meeting, including as many members of staff as possible.

The examples for the seven stages of a topic illustrate the need for staff to work together very closely. There will, of course, be other times when the topic is not suitable to contain all the work identified as necessary for progression through the curriculum. There is still a necessity for the child to be viewed as a whole and this next example shows how this can be achieved.

Example (special school)

Yazi has profound and multiple learning disabilities and has regular input from his class teacher, a nursery nurse, a physiotherapist, a speech therapist, a special teacher of the visually impaired, a dinner lady and the transport escort as well as his family. Co-ordinating this army of people is in the hands of the class teacher and it can prove very difficult to manage.

The physiotherapist wanted Yazi to have daily exercises to avoid contractures and malformations. She suggested that he should have his position changed frequently to avoid sores and to drain chest fluids which can build up in someone who cannot move independently. She also felt Yazi could be learning to sit with a little help from an adult or from a supporting chair. The long term aim would be for the support to be gradually faded until he could sit supporting himself at a table holding on to hand grips.

The speech therapist was particularly concerned with helping Yazi to eat comfortably without choking. She also wanted him to take the food from the spoon with his lips rather than receiving it passively from the person feeding. Her other concern was with his communication. As he was at a very early stage of communication his care givers needed to be very consistent in their handling of him and should keep to very simple routines. These should be repeated many times to encourage Yazi to anticipate what was going to happen next and even begin to indicate what he wanted to happen, though this was a long term aim rather than an immediate goal.

The specialist teacher of the visually impaired wanted to make use of tactile clues to enable Yazi to build up some idea of the world around him. Care givers wore bracelets made of different materials and made sure that Yazi was able to feel them and begin to identify individuals, before anyone did anything for him. Other clues were added, for example, every time he was lifted out of his chair, his arm was lifted first to warn him of what was going to happen.

Through discussion with everyone involved, the class teacher devised a programme that encompassed all the expressed priorities.

1. Daily exercises – bending and stretching all joints
                    – practise sitting balance
                    – hand function
2. A feeding programme – moving from pureed to chopped food
3. The use of tactile clues to help Yazi make sense of a world he cannot see
4. A sensory stimulation programme to encourage the best use of the senses
5. A communication programme making use of simple routines carried out by everyone in the same way
6. A positioning programme to ensure good posture and drainage

All the staff involved at any time with Yazi were introduced to all parts of the programme so that he would receive the same treatment from everyone. It was explained that as Yazi found it so difficult to communicate with the world around him, his care givers would have to become very sensitive and very skilled at interpreting any small signs he might make. Routines were very important and needed to be repeated many times.

Work with pupils with profound and multiple learning disabilities can become narrowly focused and staff have to find ways of maintaining interest whilst keeping to carefully worked out programmes. Using a topic to direct the work can be very useful, even though the pupil probably will not be aware of the change of subject. Practising sitting and holding his head in midline will remain the same for Yazi but the stimulation for this will change with the topic from listening to football songs in the Keeping Fit topic, to listening to different animal sounds in a topic about animals. (Listening will remain a useful stimuli because Yazi has no sight and he needs to use both hands to maintain his sitting position.)

Creating a collaborative curriculum

The last example featured a pupil with very complex disabilities and a large team of teachers and therapists, but the principle of working together towards common goals remains the same, however demanding the needs and whatever the size of the team. If we accept that everything in which the pupil is involved in school constitutes the curriculum, we must find ways of making this into a complete package, crossing not only subject barriers but also differences apparent in the work of specialists and therapists.

There is no suggestion that the specialist knowledge of each professional is not needed. It would be very difficult for one person to accumulate all the experience and expertise of the large team described in the example about Yazi. In fact, it may not be desirable. Different people bring different perspectives to pupils' needs and often a combination of ideas is greater than a sum of the parts. A well run team of professionals working towards a collaborative curriculum will undoubtedly offer every pupil the best of all worlds.

Class teachers, who are often the co-ordinators of multi-disciplinary teams, need to be more aware of the work of the available specialists. There can be a tendency to heave a sigh of relief when the specialist arrives which results in a shifting of all responsibility. Working together to address perceived problems within the bounds of the classroom and the curriculum offers a much more coherent package for pupils. There has been a considerable shift away from remedial programmes delivered in the broom cupboard towards an approach which focuses on adapting the curriculum to enhance the learning needs of all pupils (Hart, 1992). The role of learning support teachers has shifted from working with individual pupils to collaborating with class or subject teachers on all areas of the curriculum. This can also be seen to be happening with specialist teachers of sensory impairments. It is, however, more difficult for peripatetic staff to become intimately involved in a whole curriculum in every school and unit that they visit. It is even more difficult for therapists who do not have a detailed knowledge of curriculum matters and are employed by the health authorities to carry out paramedical tasks.

The work in this chapter has described some attempts to overcome the inherent problems in trying to create a holistic approach to the curriculum received by pupils. In advocating a system of *whole child, whole curriculum* we have demonstrated how this can be possible and although the medium suggested is cross curricular, there is no reason why the principle of placing mobility training and physiotherapy exercises within the curriculum could not happen in a more subject-ridden classroom. The final example in this chapter describes a scene in a school for pupils with physical disabilities which sums up a truly collaborative approach to the curriculum.

Example
Six children from the nursery and infant department are sitting on the red mats in the middle of the room. There are five adults present. The leader of the session is a physiotherapist and there are two classroom assistants, a speech therapy assistant and a teacher working alongside. The emphasis in this session is on rolling, reaching and sitting but the leader can be seen to produce two balls of different sizes and colours and spend some time conducting a lesson on 'big' and 'little' and 'red' and 'yellow'. Two of the children are not able to join in at this level, so she spends a few moments gaining eye contact with them, an important objective in their individual programmes.

Some of the principles of Conductive Education are being used and with the two most verbal children, the leader is encouraging a verbalisation of the exercises with sentences such as 'my head is in the middle' and 'my legs are straight'. Others are asked to touch their head or their legs, partly to improve their sitting balance and partly to reinforce body vocabulary.

The scene continues with a constant blurring at the edges between therapy and teaching. Much consultation and considerable prior effort had gone into this kind of session. Staff at this school are encouraged to make time to have meetings to discuss priorities for pupils. Staff attend each other's sessions to try to understand the curriculum from each other's perspectives and to ensure that what the children receive is a unified whole. This situation is not achieved without commitment from all involved, a determined leader and a very flexible view of staffing. Inter-disciplinary teams take time to evolve and need considerable support to flourish.

CHAPTER 5

Collaboration for Assessment

Although assessment has been mentioned several times in previous chapters, we feel that a section devoted to this subject is necessary to enable sufficient discussion of the aspects that particularly relate to support services and the curriculum. An overview of assessment in special education will be presented alongside the current scene of National Curriculum assessment. Opportunities for collaboration between professionals will be explored and ways of achieving pupil involvement in assessment will be presented as a centre-piece.

Special education and assessment

It has already been suggested that special education and educational psychology developed side by side at the beginning of the 20th century. Psychometrics had enormous importance for ascertaining placement of pupils to the extent that educational psychologists could be summed up by the term 'test-basher' (Thomas, 1989). Although this is not a wholly accurate view of educational psychologists today, they still occupy a key place in the assessment procedures surrounding pupils who are experiencing difficulties. The advice given by such professionals is highly regarded by those who are responsible for deciding upon provision and services. Teachers become, understandably, frustrated when the results of their own assessments are given less weight than those of someone who had seen the pupil perhaps once for a total of twenty minutes.

The preoccupation over the years with standardised tests was built on a view of education that could only be run efficiently if pupils were divided into groups of like ability. Educationalists have moved away from this towards a philosophy which endorses comprehensive education for all. The present government is trying to persuade us to think differently in an age of competition and market forces but the push towards creating schools that can adapt their curriculum for all pupils is still in evidence (Ainscow, 1991). It must, however, be acknowledged that we are a long way from 'inclusive education' for all pupils and special education will still have a part to play in building bridges between the curriculum and many pupils.

Our concern, at this point, is with curriculum assessment (see Part I for discussion of assessment for school placement) and special schools can be seen to have much experience in the cyclical process of assessment, curriculum planning, delivery and reassessment.

Figure 5.1   The Cyclical Process

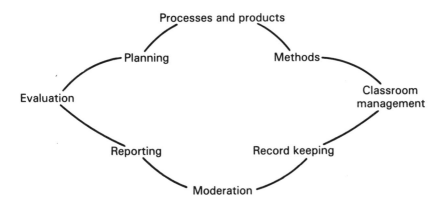

Assessment, in this cycle, can be seen to be informative and is directly related to the teaching and learning which goes on in the classroom. Many special schools and departments have invested a considerable amount of time and energy writing objectives-based curriculum statements with criteria attached from which to deliver and assess pupils' learning (Ainscow and Tweddle, 1979; Gardner *et al.,* 1983). There is a direct connection between curriculum and assessment which, through careful measurement, can indicate progression for even the most profoundly disabled pupils. It cannot be denied, though, that strict adherence to prescribed curriculum statements can lead to the acquisition of skills that can only be performed in limited circumstances and a narrow curriculum where only the easily measurable is taught (McConkey, 1981).

National Curriculum assessment

In order to understand the demands of National Curriculum assessment, it is useful to begin by considering the four purposes of assessment as set out in the TGAT Report (DES, 1987).

- Formative:
  so that the positive achievements of a pupil may be recognised and discussed and the appropriate next steps may be planned
- Diagnostic:
  through which learning difficulties may be scrutinised and classified so that appropriate remedial help and guidance can be provided
- Summative:
  for the recording of the overall achievement of a pupil in a systematic way
- Evaluative:
  by means of which some aspects of the work of a school, an LEA or other discrete part of the educational service can be assessed and/or reported upon.

(DES, 1987, para.23)

The first two purposes refer to work directly in the classroom and are designed to keep teaching and learning well matched to pupils' needs. The latter two are perhaps more controversial and refer much more to comparisons between classes, schools and LEAs. We will not be concerned much with this angle on assessment, although the presence of competition and market forces cannot completely be ignored even in a chapter about collaborative assessment in the classroom.

The TGAT Report also recommended that the curriculum be divided into 10 levels for the purposes of reporting progress. As the statutory orders for each subject have been written, this recommendation has been taken into account. Each of these 10 levels contains Statements of Attainment against which each pupil can be measured and progress plotted. Progress is seen in a somewhat linear fashion, a view which is open to question. It is hard to see all learning taking place in a conveniently hierarchical manner. This point will be taken up later in this chapter as there are considerable implications for the way in which staff conduct assessment in the way in which they view children's learning.

National assessment is, in fact, two pronged. Continuous teacher assessment is carried out by teachers using whatever methods they find useful and refers to every Attainment Target of the National Curriculum. Standard Assessment Tasks (SATs) are administered four times during a pupil's career at the ages of 7, 11, 14 and 16 and these are attached to sample Attainment Targets. Although the TGAT Report suggested that these two facets should be equal in status, SATs have become the dominant force in the eyes of many people. If the level assigned to a pupil by the teacher through teacher assessment conflicts with the result from a SAT then the statutory orders rule that the SAT should prevail (subject to enquiry at LEA level) (DES, 1990b). This rule can have important implications for pupils with special needs as they may not be able to function at a level or pace that is commensurate with the demands of the SATs.

There have been various pilot and full runs of SATs at the time of writing (October, 1992) and the difficulties and successes of pupils with SENs have been carefully collated where possible. The most significant finding is the need to modify or adapt the tasks to enable equal access to the materials and to potential success (Pearson, 1990). This can cause enormous problems of validity apart from the considerable amount of time needed by teachers and support staff to effect these modifications. Staff in schools for pupils with severe learning difficulties found they had to adapt key stage 1 SATs to the point where they wondered if they bore any resemblance to the original tasks (Fathers, 1990). A school for the blind and visually impaired found the time taken to modify materials for key stage 3 SATs, 'excessive', putting staff under considerable pressure (CATS, 1991). We will return to this point later when considering how staff can work together for the kind of support acceptable during the SAT time.

This is an opportune moment to stand back a little from conducting SATs and consider the purposes of the exercise and its effects upon pupils with SENs. One of the key concerns is with the raising of standards throughout the country. Many writers are sceptical about the way in which assessment can raise standards (Gipps, 1990). There is the old story about how you cannot make the pig heavier by continually weighing it! Assessment alone is not the answer and in the meantime, pupils with SENs will be continually under pressure for dragging standards down. This is directly related to other key concerns, those of market forces and competition. If pupils with SENs cannot contribute positively towards the results of individual schools, their presence may have a detrimental effect upon the ability of the school to attract pupils. This is a well worn argument which seems to fall on deaf ears in the Department for Education, whose solutions relate mostly to complicated disapplications and exemptions from parts of the National Curriculum.

It is easy to become thoroughly disheartened over standard assessment when considering pupils with SENs. It could be argued that our time would be better spent improving continuous assessment in the classroom so that pupil profiles can be built up and strengths and needs can be fully described to inform our daily work. Most of the rest of this chapter is devoted to this and the first consideration is concerned with how we gather evidence of pupil learning and how the different professionals working in the classroom can interpret this.

Evidence of learning

The most obvious evidence of learning is the exercise book and the child's work within it. It is equally obvious that this is only part of the story and that teachers who rely entirely on written work for assessing progress will gain a partial picture.

Work, both in mainstream and special schools, is very varied and involves pupils in many different activities, some of which include written responses but many of which require oral responses, artefacts to be made, movement sequences or music to be composed. It is a considerable challenge to teachers to make sense of all this, especially the transient evidence; the discussion about the frog spawn, the subtraction process and the negotiation over a tricky problem.

If we add to all the different kinds of the evidence, the variety in learning styles of individual pupils, the enormity of the task of making informed judgements can be appreciated. Pollard and Tann (1987) describe four sets of characteristics concerning the cognitive aspects of learning and five personality dimensions.

Aspects of learning style: cognition

Wholist (likes a grasp of the whole picture) − serialist (prefers methodically building up the picture)

Field dependent (uses a general context to solve problems − field independent (analyses problem components)

Scanning (makes initial general hypothesis and fits rest in) − focusing (looks at each part before arriving at hypothesis)

Divergent (uses inspirational flair) – convergent (needs to find the 'right answer')

Aspects of learning style: personality
Impulsivity (rushing at a task) – reflexivity (chewing it over endlessly)
Extroversion (outgoing and gregarious) – introversion (keeping to oneself)
Anxiety (anxious about work) – adjustment (accepting and satisfied)
Vacillation (short concentration spans) – perseverance (staying power)
Competitiveness (finding it hard to share) – collaborativeness (working well with others but perhaps becoming dependent)
(Pollard and Tann, 1987, pp.155–6)

Understanding children's learning is further complicated, when we are considering pupils with SENs, by the presence of the many different professionals. Each specialist has not only a set of published tests related specifically to the learning connected with their own specialism, but also a set of preconceived ideas and beliefs built upon their own training and experience. It is an enormously complicated job to co-ordinate all this without spending vast amounts of time in meetings to discuss the progress of individual pupils on a daily basis.

Whichever way you look at it, staff involved in special education have a complex task as they sort out the needs, the strengths, the weaknesses and the next appropriate steps for each and every pupil in their care. This prompts them to use a variety of methods and to organise the classroom in diverse ways. In the same classroom children may be working alone, in pairs, in small groups or as a whole class. Trying to evolve ways in which to collect evidence of learning through all this can be a daunting prospect. There is certainly more to it than marking exercise books. There is more to it than looking at the product of learning.

Staff have got to be able to observe and make judgements about the processes as well. It is only by looking at the way in which pupils tackle problems and by listening to their explanations and questions that a true picture of learning can be obtained. The context needs to be taken into account, the 'hidden agenda' explored and pre-judgements kept to a minimum. For many staff this is a new area of their work. There are new skills to be gained, new concepts to be understood and new attitudes to be found.

Evidence

Trying to define the nature of evidence is a good place to begin. When asked about this, teachers in mainstream and special schools listed evidence as, scribble, talk, pictures, models, writing, drawing, project reports, artefacts, behaviour, videos, photographs, computer printouts, answers to questions and the word of another adult. The list is almost endless.

There are some publications which can help to define the kind of evidence that staff might want to seek. The *Primary Language Record* (Barrs *et al.*, 1988) is particularly useful with its 'Observations and Samples' proforma. The guidelines suggest, for example, that all different kinds of talk should be recorded in diary form. The authors suggest that examples could include:

- planning an event;
- solving a problem;
- expressing a point of view or feelings;
- telling a story.

There is also advice on possible learning contexts and social contexts that could reveal different kinds of talk. This kind of guidance covers reading and writing as well, and although the original Record was compiled before the National Curriculum appeared, it has since been up-dated (Barrs *et al.*, 1990). The up-date, however, has not included changing the shape of the Record to include statements of attainment as the authors advocate a holistic approach to assessment which would be difficult to achieve if it was divided into small chunks.

Many staff compile their own proforma for relevant evidence of learning. The following example is taken from a primary school and involves a support teacher conducting an assessment session with a group of eight Year 1 pupils.

Example
At a full team meeting, Mrs Jones, the support teacher, had contributed to the drawing up of a record sheet for the latest topic which was about 'People we know'. The team of four (three class teachers for Years 1 and 2 and the support teacher)

had agreed they would use six categories to help their thinking. There would be three levels to accommodate the diversity of ability demonstrated by the pupils. Level A contained the following 'I can do' statements:

1. Personal Development: I can talk about my work to a friend
2. Observation and Classification: I can make sets about different jobs
3. Particular Language: I know about these words: milkman, postman, fireman, policeman
4. Communication: I can draw pictures about my work and write under the teacher's words
5. Enquiry: I can ask a question
6. Empathy: I can pretend to be a policeman

The members of the team decided that most of the assessment could be conducted whilst they were working normally, but that if the children were going to be able to complete their own record sheets, time would have to be set aside for this. Mrs Jones was to be a key figure in this, as she could provide an independent and corroborating pair of eyes during the observation of normal class work as well as working with specific groups of children on their own record sheet.

Mrs Jones had a small group of eight pupils, all with a level A topic record sheet. They all sat round a table and joined together in a short discussion about the sheet and its demands. Some of the session involved simple questions and answers but there was a chance for everyone to join in a short improvisation about an accident which involved bringing in imaginary emergency services. By the end of the forty minutes, categories 3, 4 and 6 had been covered and each child had short sentences and/or drawings on their record sheet. Mrs Jones completed each sheet with an evaluation of her own, which was one, two or three sides of a triangle depending upon how well she felt the child had managed. She discussed this with each child as she drew the session to a close.

As she gave the record sheet to the teacher, Mrs Jones briefly recounted the highlights of the lesson. She shared her relief that one child had managed much better than she feared and that another child would need particular help with letter formation before the wrong orientation became ingrained. Both teachers made a note of this for immediate action.

One of the most important things about this last example, is the involvement of the pupils in their own record-keeping. They had been part of the whole procedure. They knew what evidence was being collected and were consulted about the teacher evaluation during the session. Although they did not necessarily understand the language of the six categories chosen by the teachers, they certainly understood the 'I can do' statements and thoroughly enjoyed demonstrating what they could do and understand.

All too often, pupils are not part of the assessment procedure. It is something done *to* them rather than *with* them. Whilst carrying out some research on assessment in primary classrooms, we asked pupils what they thought the teacher was looking for in a piece of good work. Top juniors in one school answered: 'finishing quickly', 'not messy', 'doing what she says', 'answering the question', 'good writing', 'the way it's set out'. One pupil mentioned the points system in use in the classroom at this time. On being pressed a little about the content of their pieces of work, so far unmentioned, one pupil suggested that the teacher might be looking for 'rhyming words' and another tentatively said 'adventure?'

These pupils clearly felt that the evidence that the teacher was looking for was almost exclusively concerned with the way it looked. The teacher, herself, was very disappointed with the answers given by her pupils. She felt that she had spent considerable time making clear what she wanted, which definitely included vocabulary, storyline and invention.

This is not an unusual occurrence, pupils will give the evidence they 'think' is wanted by the teacher. If they can get a 'star' by producing a page of neat writing, spelled correctly within the time allotted, they will not spend much time on content. By the same token, it is difficult for a pupil with imagination to gain one of these 'stars' if his or her handwriting is poor or spelling inaccurate. In fact the assessment arrangements for the Writing Profile in the National Curriculum does little to acknowledge this, as the level given to pupils depends upon a combination of the three Attainment Targets, Writing, Spelling and Handwriting (DES, 1990a).

It appears that staff must be far less coy with pupils about what evidence they are looking for in their work. The teacher who gives the children farm animals to make counting work fun will only get genuine counting if s/he makes this clear. If the instructions to the children are about playing with the animals then this is likely to be the outcome and the evidence of counting will not be there (Bennett and Kell, 1989). If pupils are more fully aware of what evidence is being sought, the collecting will be much easier on both sides.

Questioning

One of the most useful skills for all staff seeking to gain evidence of children's learning is that of effective questioning. It has been discussed by many educators. For example, Perrott (1982) suggests that it may be the most important activity in which teachers engage (p.41). He cites the results of many researchers which seem to suggest that teachers can ask as many as four hundred questions a day. Floyd (1960), Perrott tells us, found that of the 348 questions a day he heard, 75 per cent needed specific answers. Other writers have suggested that relying too heavily upon such lower order questions can actually place too much emphasis on learning that is concerned with pure memory rather than on encouraging more thoughtful and complete answers demonstrating the manipulation of information for a purpose.

Pollard and Tann (1987) divide pedagogical questions into 'closed' and 'open', suggesting that closed questions have a low-level cognitive demand. They go on to say that the form of questioning needed at any one time by the teacher depends very much on the purpose intended. Sometimes a mono-syllabic answer reveals the evidence needed for crediting the pupil with knowledge or understanding but at other times more open-ended questions may reveal much more about the way in which the pupil is functioning and much more about the level she or he has reached.

Kerry (1982, p.16) suggests there are nine different question types:

1. data recall
2. naming
3. observation
4. control
5. pseudo-questions
6. speculative or hypothesis generating
7. reasoning or analysis
8. evaluation
9. problem solving

Question types 1−5 are less demanding than questions 6−9 and skilful staff can use the sequence to build up from lower to higher to make progressive demands on pupils' thinking.

The next example is taken from the observation of a reception class teacher assessing a pupil's grasp of a science topic on frogs and tadpoles.

Example

Miss Price called small groups of three or four children over to the aquarium which was full of tadpoles and tiny frogs. She had two magnifying glasses and a microscope with observation dishes for the children to use. The topic had been pursued for several weeks and this was a chance to attempt a more formal assessment than had been possible during that time. She had decided which vocabulary and concepts to check and roughly the kinds of questions she needed to ask. This was the sequence of questions asked of one pupil and their classification according to Kerry.

What are you going to look through?	1. data recall
What can you see here?	3. observation
Can you tell me what you can see?	3. observation
Are they the same?	3. observation
Can you remember what they are?	1. data recall
Where did we take some of our tadpoles?	2. naming
What can you see them doing?	3. observation
Which bit is wiggling a lot?	1. data recall
Why does it scare you?	7. reasoning
What do you think it's going to do to you?	6. speculative
What are these going to change into?	1. data recall
Why are you moving that? (the focus on the microscope)	7. reasoning
What does it do when you move this?	7. reasoning
Can I look?	genuine question
What's happened, what does it make it do?	7. reasoning

She is indeed making a progression from closed to open questions although the majority (9 out of 15) can be seen to be of a lower order.

Interestingly, on another occasion, Miss Price decided not to ask questions at all. She was assessing the pupils' skills and understanding of simple sequences of patterns. She sat on the floor with various pieces of apparatus and began to make her own patterns. Children joined her and soon were industriously making their own. She mused quietly about what she was doing and introduced certain ideas and the children mused alongside. After the session, she was able to record a considerable amount of information about the skills and understanding of the group she was with. Some pupils had been particularly inventive and there is no doubt in her mind that the information revealed during this exercise fulfilled her expectations and also showed other possibilities which she had not considered.

Sometimes, therefore, it is not necessary to ask questions to find out what children can do, understand or feel strongly about. Setting up situations and observing what is happening can be extremely revealing.

Observation

Observation is not, however, an easy alternative to direct questioning. If two people observe five minutes of activity from one particular pupil, a comparison of notes will probably reveal that even if they had agreed on what to look for, they will have very different things recorded. It is notoriously difficult to observe everything and even more difficult to agree on what was seen. This does not necessarily mean that the exercise is not valid. In fact, we suggest that joint observations producing collaborative data can be very powerful.

First, let us consider some of the ways in which observations can be organised. Observation schedules are usually associated with research and much has been written about unstructured and structured, participant and non-participant observation, time and event sampling and other such procedures (Cohen and Manion, 1989; Woods, 1986; Burgess, 1985). On the whole, structured schedules are not associated with general classroom work as they are difficult to operate, especially if it involves precise timing. However, it is not impossible to create schedules that are usable in terms of time and useful in terms of data collected.

The *Primary Language Record* already referred to, offers an optional observation and sample sheet. There are suggestions that some recording of observation needs to take place at least once or twice a term 'in order to build up a good continuous picture of development' (Barrs *et al.*, 1988, p.36). Referring to reading and writing, the authors suggest that staff, looking back over cumulative observation, will be able to see where support is needed. The prompt offered to the teacher concerning the reading diary of observation is:'Record observations of the child's development as a reader (including wider experiences of stories) across a range of contexts' (Barrs *et al.*, 1988, Record Sheet). Other prompts are available in the handbook which include things such as: 'how the child responds to books and the world of print − how the child chooses and uses books and materials for different reading purposes' (p.40). Although this does not overtly tell staff how to observe, the prompts help them to succeed in the interpretations of what has been seen and also to ensure that the right kinds of experiences have been available for the pupils. A single score data concerning reading, such as a reading age or a tick against a reading level, is largely inappropriate as it adds little to the teacher's knowledge about the nature and quality of children's reading. Checklists can be helpful as they go some way towards recording the complexity of learning to read, but they suffer from being prescriptions of how the author thinks children ought to behave. A true record should include observations and samples of work as well as the pupil's eye view (Pearson, 1988).

Creating a list of prompts for observation can be invaluable. These are less prescriptive than checklists but can give direction and help to ensure progression through the curriculum. The next example is a prompt list put together by a teacher wanting to assess language work at levels 1−5 in the National Curriculum.

Prompt Sheet for Speaking and Listening levels 1−5

child as conversationalist
child as listener
communication strategies
responses to literature
understanding and giving instructions
asking and answering questions
child as a group member

learning strategies
knowledge about language
planning and taking part in presentations

It can be seen immediately, that this is considerably more powerful than a simple checklist. It can lead to very useful discussion concerning the way in which the curriculum is presented.

Example
The staff of one special school spent many curriculum meetings discussing suitable prompts for keeping records for their mathematics curriculum. They had a long history of recording skills and had a highly developed system for dating and ticking specified objectives. There was a gradual realisation that there was no mechanism for recording pupils' understanding nor their development of knowledge about things mathematical.

The following is an example of one of the sheets that was devised to give help to staff involved. The lists are by no means complete but are offered to encourage further thought.

Counting
Skills
  C1 Counts by rote 1-3
  C2 Counts by rote 1-5
  C3 Counts by rote 1-10
  C4 Counts objects 1-3 when they are in a line or grouped for easy counting
  C5 Counts objects 1-5 when they are in a line or grouped for easy counting
  C6 Counts objects 1-10 when they are in a line or grouped for easy counting
  C7 Counts objects 1-10 grouping them for easy counting as s/he goes

Understanding
Observe the understanding demonstrated by the child. Record exactly what you judge to be the level of understanding of the concept of counting. Be specific with objects/circumstances/language/limitations.

Suggested areas: rote counting

a)   offers counting when asked 'how many' even if inaccurate at first

b)   counts along with the group in counting songs and rhymes

c)   counts as part of hide and seek and stories such as 'The Three Little Pigs'

Suggested areas: counting objects

a)   counts out objects to make sure there are enough for everyone

b)   plays counting games with counters and spot dice

c)   fetches correct number of cutlery/pencils/books etc. in normal class life

d)   demonstrates an understanding that the number you finish on is the number of objects counted and you only count each object once

Knowledge

Look for this kind of knowledge and be specific for each child:

a)   knows that numbers are involved in birthdays/where you live/shopping/eating/sweets etc.

b)   knows own address and age

c)   knows a repertoire of number rhymes, songs and stories

Collecting data using these prompts meant that no longer were the objectives sheets sufficient to record what the pupils were doing. New sheets had to be devised to add to them and there was no way of avoiding a narrative manner of recording. The sheets used were purposely divided into small areas so that records could be brief and to-the-point. It is well documented that long records are read by no-one.

Some of the evidence collected became outdated and could be superseded, so it was decided that the summary sheet would be annotated each half term only. Short-term progress could be plotted through individual teachers' notebooks and planning diaries and longer-term progress could be seen in the summary sheet and eventually, the annual review.

Staff were now looking further than mere skills acquisition for their records. They were discussing with colleagues, their individual and collective judgements of pupils' understanding and were agreeing on their own sets of prompts while collecting evidence.

Dynamic assessment

Before we move on to considering how best to carry out assessment in a collaborative manner, it will be useful to consider an important view of assessment which emanates from the United States and pupils with mild or moderate learning difficulties.

Campione (1989) writes of the limitations of standard, static assessment which seems more likely to misclassify students and give a negative view of their performance than to contribute to diagnosis and inform intervention. He recommends a different kind of assessment that he calls 'dynamic'. The emphasis is more on process than on product and the interest is in the embryonic skills demonstrated by pupils as they begin the next step in their learning. Campoine refers to Vygotsky's 'zone of proximal development' in which pupils can show the start of new thinking. If this is measured through finding out how much assistance is needed to complete a task then the information available will enable future tasks to be more closely matched to the learner.

One researcher in this area, Feuerstein (cited in Campoine, 1989) has developed simple paper and pencil exercises called 'Instrumental Enrichment' which brings assessment and instruction close together. These exercises are rather removed from usual class activities so that transfer of learning is not proven. Campoine, however, suggests the need for a great deal of interaction between teacher and learner as they move through possible ways in which the student can be assisted to understand what is required.

So often assessment is a matter of black and white. What the pupil does and does not know or can and cannot do. Dynamic assessment encourages staff to look at that 'grey area in between' and assess what children can do with assistance. Vygotsky referred to this as the 'gap' which exists for an individual between what he or she can do alone and what can be achieved with help from one more knowledgeable or skilled. If that 'gap' is observed and the assistance is analysed then there will be a much more accurate picture built up of immediate need for learning to progress (Wood, 1988). The following example demonstrates how a simple analysis of the amount of support needed by a pupil can be used in practice. The pupil is much involved in the process and is even helped to provide some of her own support strategies.

Example

After several weeks of Mary arriving late for lessons with the wrong books, no homework and a general feeling of disorganisation, the support teacher, Mr Jones decided it was time to take the situation in hand. He asked her subject teachers for their experiences and he sat down to talk to Mary to find out what the problem was all about. He quickly discovered that she had lost her timetable and even when she had had it she did not remember to consult it when packing her bag. Everyone at home was very busy in the morning so it was difficult for her to get help in organising her life. She also had a poor internal map of the school and was always getting lost.

Mr Jones devised several strategies for helping Mary to arrive on time for lessons with the correct equipment. One was to attach a timetable in a plastic folder to her bag. On the back of the timetable was a simple checklist of things she needed for each day. Other strategies involved simple written and verbal reminders from various people within the school and one or two well-placed signs which she made herself to help her move between lessons.

Three weeks later Mr Jones assessed the situation, consulting with various members of staff after asking for their observations. He asked particularly for them to be specific about the kind of help Mary still needed to arrive correctly equipped. The results of their observations were considered and Mr Jones and Mary formulated the next stage of the programme so that she could proceed to become a little more responsible for her own strategies.

Collaborative assessment

Consulting or working collaboratively with other professionals can add considerably to the validity of data collected through questioning and observation. Apart from the knowledge and experience that each person can bring to the situation, everyone sees something different which, in its turn, can contribute to the whole picture.

Staff in special education and in nursery education have spent many years building up an ideal of multi-disciplinary assessment. On many occasions that has meant much overlap as different professionals assess the same things in the same child. Just imagine how many times aspects of communication are assessed by teachers, speech therapists, nursery nurses, health visitors, hearing specialists etc. How much more sensible for there to be a united approach by assessors. At the very least there should be agreement on what is being assessed and the methods to be used. Ideally there should be opportunities for joint observation or individual observation of the same child, so that judgements can be checked and particular specialisms brought to bear upon the strengths and needs presented by the child.

Many staff who work with older pupils are used to being alone in the classroom and are unused to having their judgements questioned or even challenged. They find this part of collaborative work particularly threatening (Blenkin and Kelly, 1992). Although those who work in special schools or in nursery situations are probably more used to having other adults around, it is quite rare for classroom assessment to be carried out by anyone other than the teacher. Specialists tend to arrive and withdraw children for particular tests and then return them with, perhaps, the promise of a report at a later date.

True collaboration between professionals entails discussion about the types of assessment necessary and an agreement about who will carry it out. If everyone in contact with the child is working on the same programmes then, theoretically, anyone in the team can carry out valid assessments.

Example

Mr Knight, a class teacher, worked very closely with Mrs Wish, a speech and language therapist. Although Mrs Wish did withdraw two pupils for specific articulation work, the majority of her time was spent in the classroom working alongside the teacher and pupils. When the pupils, who had moderate learning difficulties, went swimming or to PE lessons, she accompanied them and carried out her work during whatever curriculum experience they were receiving. Sometimes in the classroom, she worked with groups of children in areas of general language development.

At the beginning of term, Mr Knight and Mrs Wish met to discuss suitable categories for collecting data concerning the language progress of the pupils. They devised a simple sheet which they then shared with all other staff who came in contact with the pupils. Although everyone knew what was expected, it was the responsibility of the teacher and therapist to draw the attention of other staff to the record and invite them to contribute to it. Observations were shared throughout the term and samples of language were collected. Mr Knight used the evidence to compile a brief summary and bring the master record sheets up-to-date. This was then agreed with Mrs Wish and the next steps were discussed. An end-of-term whole team meeting was the forum for sharing the effectiveness of this procedure.

If staff are to work collaboratively in the area of assessment, then time must be set aside for this to happen. Initially this might take up a considerable amount of time but as understanding between staff increases, the discussions can become less frequent.

SATs and support services

Although it is not the intention in this chapter to spend much time on Standard Assessment Tasks, it will be useful to consider the role of support services in carrying them out as that has potential implications for any assessment procedures. The tests themselves are set and standard but the presentation and modifications necessary for individual pupils varies according to need and staff need to be aware of the demands made on them during the time set aside for conducting SATs.

The Report by the Consortium for Assessment and Testing in School (CATS) on the 1991 key stage 3 pilot SATs reveal some interesting facts and opinions which can give a few pointers towards how staff can work together effectively. These will be summarised.

- Support staff need training to familiarise themselves with the materials in order to support pupils effectively during the SAT period.
- Significant time is required to make the modifications necessary.
- Guidance needs to refer specifically to modifications as well as subject matter.
- Too much modification of materials could call into question the validity of the standardisation of the task.
- Consultation with support staff is necessary before the choice of SAT is made so that its suitability can be checked (e.g. a SAT is not chosen that relies totally on an ability to hear when there are hearing impaired pupils in the group).

- Support staff need to be very sensitive to pupils getting bored with a SAT which it is taking them a long time to complete. Extra time may be allowed to compensate for a particular disability but this can lead to frustration.
- Support staff must be aware of the possibility of over prompting pupils whilst helping to reduce feelings of failure.

(CATS, 1991)

There are many other results from the pilot reported by CATS but we have highlighted those that actually refer to staff involvement rather than to the tasks themselves. It appears that close collaboration between subject and support staff during SATs is vital to ensure that all pupils have the best opportunity to demonstrate their abilities and achievements. If this is normal experience then the biggest problem will be the enormous amount of time it takes to modify materials rather than any of the principles of working together.

Joint record-keeping

The final concern of this chapter is with joint record-keeping. Many schools, both mainstream and special, are struggling to find answers to the problem of how to make record-keeping quick to complete yet revealing of progress. There is little evidence that joint record-keeping across specialisms and disciplines features very highly in this struggle. Even the special school, which has been used to provide several examples in this book, has not advanced much in this area despite appointing a member of senior staff as responsible for multi-disciplinary collaboration.

It will be useful to consider the purposes of record-keeping as we try to understand the problems and conceive of possible solutions. A good place to start is with Rance in 1971 who begins his list of seven reason for keeping records with: records are kept

> to assess what has been achieved in the past, and to show the rate of progress at present and the direction in which the overall development of a school's education is moving.

(Rance, 1971, p.14)

He goes on to enumerate:

- recording individual progress;
- comparing academic achievement;

- diagnosing problems;
- facilitating transfer;
- promoting co-operation between schools.

Almost twenty years later, SEAC (1990) refers to Circular 17/89 and the first purpose for record-keeping they cite is: 'To record the Attainment Targets and Statements of Attainment which each pupil has attempted' (p.60).

This section continues with reference to achievement levels, progress, evidence and reporting to parents. This is very much in the vocabulary surrounding the National Curriculum and its demands for assessment, and it demonstrates how thinking has changed over the intervening years. Whilst Rance might talk about co-operation between schools, National Curriculum-speak refers to competition and allowing market forces to boost successful schools and discard those which are unsuccessful.

Whatever the underlying political feelings, good record-keeping and its concomitant planning are essential if continuity and progression can be assured for individual pupils. It is all too easy to miss vital information about needs and strengths if no formal records are kept. It is especially important to keep written records when more than one person is involved in the education of individual pupils such as we find in special education. Very often, if they are even kept, these records are separate and belong only to the professional or service from which they originate. They may not even be shared for the annual review of the Statement of Special Educational Need. In the light of this, there needs to be a much greater openness concerning records, particularly those with which we are most concerned in this chapter, curriculum records.

Blenkin and Kelly (1992) offer some useful principles underlying teacher assessment and record-keeping and we summarise these here.

1. Teacher assessment and record-keeping are part of normal work in the classroom. They are ongoing and cumulative.
2. They are holistic in that they record the learning process as a whole rather than just an end product.
3. All those involved in the children's learning are involved in the assessments and records.
4. Children understand clearly what is expected of them when assessments are being made.
5. Teacher assessment takes account of equal opportunities in terms of gender, race, class and special needs.

6. Records are linked to planning to ensure progression and balance.
7. Children's progress cannot be reduced to checklists and rows of numbers.
8. Assessment and record-keeping are based on samples of work produced and observation made.

Records of Achievement

In the introduction to this chapter, it was stated that a central feature would be the involvement of pupils in their own assessment. Some of the examples used in earlier sections have already illustrated how this can happen. Records of Achievement and profiling are specifically based upon the view of pupils as partners in a process which encompasses both assessment and the curriculum upon which it is based. Profiles are a way of life and are not records bolted on to an existing curriculum. They build into a personal and positive record which reflects the concept of assessment as both process and product (Broadfoot, 1987). Pupils are helped to identify short-term educational and personal goals which are both challenging and achievable and the results accumulate into a profile to which they, the pupils, have contributed and which reflects achievement of various kinds.

The RANSC Report (DES, 1989c) recommended the introduction of a national scheme for Records of Achievement in secondary schools but unfortunately this has not been taken up in the round of educational changes brought about by the 1988 Education Reform Act. The Secretary of State at the time felt that teachers would be overburdened if they were addressing statutory Records of Achievement as well as the National Curriculum and its assessment. Despite this unfortunate, but probably correct view, many schools, primary, secondary and special, have developed their own systems. They feel strongly that the principles behind profiling are so important that the amount of time invested in their development is time well spent.

The next example is one sheet from a record devised for a group of pupils with severe learning difficulties, illustrating how imaginative staff can be when trying to involve pupils with limited language skills.

Example

Figure 5.2   Record Sheet

Things I can do by myself -

I can take off
my coat   ☐

I can put on
my coat   ☐

I can take myself
to the toilet   ☐

I can wash and
dry my hands   ☐

Source: NCC, 1992, p.22.

This particular publication is a good source of more ideas on pupil involvement in record-keeping in special schools, as is Lawson (1992) *Practical Record Keeping in Special Schools*.

It is important to get record-keeping into perspective. Many staff are feeling pressurised into devising complex and time-consuming practices which involve recording anything and everything. It really is not necessary. If everything a pupil does is recorded it begins to devalue the worth of the record. There are many snippets of information which staff may note, either physically or 'in the head' which can be used for immediate planning and then cast aside. Not everything needs to be kept.

Example
Mrs L. has a notebook which is always available for jotting short notes which serve as reminders for weekly planning. It is

available for all staff who work with her group of pupils. Each page is divided into two so that space for notes on four children can be found at a glance and the space kept small to encourage the briefest of notes. It can be used at any convenient moment. The notes are not a permanent record and when the book is full, it is not retained.

A further notebook is available at certain times agreed by the staff team. This contains specific prompts jointly decided in advance which influence the evidence sought in identified areas of learning. There is a flap which opens to the left. This contains the suggestions about what to look for. It is *not* a checklist so the prompts are open-ended (see earlier example of prompts for recording).

Each page is divided into two lengthwise so that again, notes on individual pupils are short and succinct.

Information of importance from either of these books is transferred to permanent records, either by pupils themselves in a session set aside for this purpose or by the team co-ordinator. Unusual events are discussed at the weekly planning meeting of the core team (Mrs L. and Mrs M., teacher and support teacher). The permanent set of records for each child reflects the need for plotting progress through the National Curriculum Attainment Targets as well as details of individual learning processes and samples of work. The records are summarised termly.

A good record reflects something of importance and that does not happen every day for every child. It also reflects different aspects of pupils' work. To do this, it will contain sections which record:

a) experiences
b) skills mastered
c) understanding reached
d) knowledge gained
e) attitudes demonstrated

As it is notoriously difficult for any one record to fulfil both formative and summative purposes at once (Murphy, 1988; Campbell, 1989; Barrs *et al.,* 1990), then there will be separate sections which summarise progress at particular key moments. These will probably be related to end of terms or half terms and statutory annual reviews in the case of pupils with a Statement of Special Educational Needs.

In order to develop a record-keeping system which fulfils the criteria both of being informative and succinct, a team of staff will need to ask themselves questions such as:

- How will each pupils' record be divided? Will it be in sections for different staff or will everyone contribute to the same parts?
- How will the necessary variety of records be presented?
- Where will the records be kept?
- Who will have access to the records?
- How often will they be annotated?
- Who is responsible for which section?
- What kind of evidence of learning is acceptable?
- How are they going to be collected/stored/summarised?
- Which questions will be suitable for collecting which data?
- What specific observations will need to be made?
- How often will they be made?
- How will they be organised?
- What 'prompts' are going to be used to influence evidence collecting?
- What moderation procedures are there for agreeing criteria and assessment results?
- Who needs the written records and how will this affect the way in which they are presented?
- How far are the pupils involved in their own records?
- How are parents involved?
- How are other professionals involved?
- What happens to the records when they are superseded?
- What do receiving staff find most useful?
- How often is the whole process reviewed?

Although many suggestions have been made about the practicalities of assessment and record-keeping, this subject cannot be left without recognising the enormity of the task facing staff in education in the 1990s. In mainstream schools, the sheer numbers of pupils coupled with all the National Curriculum Statements of Attainment mean that the job is impossible to do well without a nervous breakdown. The amount of detail needed for pupils with a complexity of special needs creates problems in special schools even though the number of pupils is often much smaller. The news is not good for anyone! It is helpful to keep reminding ourselves that the National Curriculum and its attendant assessment are still *experiments*. At the time of writing (October 1992), the Secretary of

State is even now asking for a re-examination of various aspects of the orders. He may make it worse, but on the other hand, things may improve. Whatever happens to statutory demands, teacher assessment in the classroom is of vital importance and all staff working with pupils with special educational needs must continue to develop good but realistic practice.

Part III

Management and Training

CHAPTER 6

Working in Teams

An introduction to teamwork

There are some tasks that one person, working in isolation, cannot do. Such a task is to support children with special needs and their families. The sheer complexity of need coupled with the way in which services are constructed in this country make it impossible for any one person to manage this task alone. Effective teamwork can lead to better service provision, increased energy and progression and greater job satisfaction. A well co-ordinated team can, in many cases, lead to better use of individual skills and more effective implementation of resources especially when there is a danger of duplication or of children 'slipping through the net'.

For many years the world of industry has recognised the importance of team work and has as a matter of routine sent staff on courses to be more effective team members and to develop the skills of personnel identified as having the potential to be 'team leaders'. With the increased acceptance that senior management team members within schools require additional skills to those of a 'good class teacher', courses are being offered which cover management qualities. Within such courses 'team building or team development' is frequently covered and course participants begin to recognise their various qualities and characteristics which can be enhanced to enable effective contributions to their school teams.

Although this type of training is beginning to be available to senior managers in schools, there is very little on offer for 'ordinary team members'. There are even fewer courses for people to work in teams that span different disciplines or specialisms. We are in no doubt that such training is the way forward in meeting the needs of children who have learning difficulties and therefore this chapter goes into some depth about the nature of teams, team building, leadership of teams, interpersonal skills, working together and achieving and maintaining team work in special education. We have drawn upon materials produced by industry in addition to those available through education services.

Different kinds of teams

The word 'team' is a very overworked term in education. We hear of 'support teams', 'curriculum teams', 'phase teams', senior management teams', 'multi-disciplinary teams' and so on. In many cases the word 'team' seems to be a misnomer. They fall into the category suggested by Payne (1982) of 'work groups'.

> A work group exists when people are brought into relationship with one another by virtue of the fact that they work together; but they do not share work tasks or responsibility, and they do not use the fact that they work together to enhance the work that they are doing.
>
> (Payne, 1982, p.5)

Payne contrasts this with a description of the type of collaborative team that is the subject of this book. He quotes Brill's definition.

> A team is a group of people, each of whom possesses particular expertise; each of whom is responsible for making individual decisions; who together hold a common purpose; who meet together to communicate, collaborate, and consolidate knowledge, from which plans are made, actions determined and future decisions influenced.
>
> (Brill, 1976, in Payne, 1982, p.22)

Payne goes on to suggest that there are many teams that fall between these two extremes, who are neither loose work groups nor fully fledged collaborative teams. He feels that these are legitimate states to be in, especially when one considers the external pressures under which groups of people work. It is sometimes impossible for teams to be fully collaborative, perhaps because they meet only fleetingly or the members are also members of many other teams and it would be impossible to be working in a fully collaborative manner with each one. This is often the case in special education and despite our call for collaboration, we do recognise the difficulties under which many teams work.

Example
Mrs P. is a physiotherapist and works at School A for two days a week and School B for two half days a week. She also

visits children at Schools C, D and E on a rotation basis to advise on equipment and mobility. In all five schools she works with several different members of staff which means that she belongs to an enormous number of different teams. If she attended team meetings in every school, she would do nothing else, so she has to select how she uses her time. In these circumstances it is very difficult to maintain a high level of collaboration with everyone, compromises have to be made and different levels of collaboration need to be achieved with each possible team.

What is teamwork?

Teamwork is about individuals working together to accomplish more than they could alone. Moreover it can be an exciting, satisfying and enjoyable undertaking. Teams, however, should not be seen as the 'universal panacea' for all tasks (Hogg, 1990). Where there is only one correct solution an individual may be able to achieve more in a shorter time. Where team work is not only desirable but essential, is in times of meeting complex needs. It is the synergy of collaborative working which makes it the most effective way forward, in essence 'the whole is greater than the sum of the individual parts'.

Handy (1985) suggests that teams are organisationally useful for the following:

- distribution of work: bringing together of skills
- problem solving/decision making
- information and idea collection/information processing
- co-ordinating and liaising between individuals and between groups
- management and control of work
- testing and ratifying decisions
- increased commitment and involvement

(Handy, 1985, pp.155–6)

In the light of this list, it could certainly be suggested that a team of two or more people working alongside a child/young person and family can form a powerful system for meeting identified needs. Getting a team to work together takes time and the dynamics within teams is usually very complex. Parents will not always find it easy to become part of a team of professionals and consequently will need guidance in understanding some of the dynamics.

Increased understanding for everyone begins with an examination of both good and bad teamwork. Perhaps, as with most things, it is easier to start with the bad than the good, so let us begin with some of the symptoms of bad teamwork.

Bad teamwork

The following list has been compiled from various sources (Knight and Bowers, 1985; Payne, 1982; Dyer, 1977; Rowntree, 1989).

- frustration due to lack of a clear vision or common purpose;
- grumbling and backbiting usually in corridors or lavatories;
- retaliations and punishment for mistakes;
- unhealthy competition — factions or cliques;
- unfair distribution of work;
- sour facial expressions and clock watching;
- poor communication between members (I never know what's going on);
- a dread of meetings;
- lack of trust in or fear of the motives of those in management positions;
- no time for development.

The list could continue, but its not a good idea to be negative for too long! You will, however, be a very lucky person if you have never worked in a school where at least some of these symptoms can be found. It takes considerable courage and expertise to counteract this kind of atmosphere and it can be very depressing for the lone worker who is longing to be part of an effective team.

Effective teams

When considering the qualities of good teams, there is much agreement between the various writers in industry and the human services. There will exist variables for each team and each individual, but the majority of characteristics can be seen in most circumstances.

A good team leader

As with any team, be it sport, an army patrol, a large corporation or voluntary agency, there needs to be a leader who can give direction and mould the individual parts into a whole. The most effective teams known to us are those that have clear leaders or heads of service who, although may employ a collegial style of management, recognise that the 'buck' stops with them and that as team leaders they have to make the final decision in an attempt to make their teams successful. Those team leaders who are prepared to be adaptable and flexible and take on any role are those who gain the respect of the other team members. For example, the head of service who will take his or her turn at making the coffee for a team meeting, or change the nappy of a child who is profoundly handicapped will be seen as someone who is part of, not apart from, the team. A good team leader will be aware of the strengths and weaknesses of each team member and will be sensitive to, and deal with, any jealousies or conflicts that may arise which could prove harmful or destructive to collaborative working.

There will be more discussion concerning leadership later in the chapter, where it will be recognised that team leaders are often individuals who have no specific power and authority over other team members and in this case perform more of a co-ordinating role.

A supportive internal environment

Individual differences are bound to exist within teams. A supportive team will acknowledge and respect these differences so that team members feel free to discuss their opinions without fear of being ridiculed or criticised. No one member will feel that their contribution is more or less important than the contributions made by others.

Working within Halpin 'open climate' (in Hoyle, 1988) should be the goal of effective teams. This is defined in terms of eight dimensions which resulted from a study undertaken by Halpin into the ways in which schools function as organisations. The most favourable climate found by these researchers was called the 'open climate' and is characterised by:

Individual staff members
low *disengagement* (individuals are thoroughly interested in and enjoy their work)
low *intimacy* (individuals do not need to be socially intimate as their working relationship is professional)
high *esprit* (individuals experience high morale and job satisfaction)

low *hindrance* (individuals don't often experience unnecessary paperwork or meetings which interfere with their work)

Leaders
high *thrust* (leaders work hard and efficiently as an example to individuals)
high *consideration* (leaders consider the professional and personal needs of individuals)
low *production emphasis* (leaders do not need to goad individuals to keep working as they are highly motivated)
low *aloofness* (leaders can work directly alongside individuals and share responsibility)

(Halpin in Hoyle, 1988, p.32)

Although this kind of climate may seem very difficult to achieve, it really has been found to be the most productive and satisfying, with all members feeling valued and able to function to the optimum degree.

Mutual trust

Information will be shared and discussed within teams which is often confidential. Team members need to feel secure in the knowledge that items discussed between each other will not be revealed in other fora. This is especially applicable in teams where parents are members, and in a truly collaborative system the family of the child with special needs is a full member.

Confidentiality is a difficult aspect of teamwork, especially if members come from different disciplines. The Health Service has long had a tradition for complete confidentiality and, at times this has resulted in frustration on the part of teachers, who often find they are debarred from vital information. After the Maria Colwell case, there has been much debate over the sharing of information between professionals in cases of child abuse. A guide for inter-agency work over child protection under the Children Act 1989 includes the following paragraphs:

Ethical and statutory codes concerned with confidentiality and data protection are not intended to prevent the exchange of information between professional staff who have a responsibility for ensuring the protection of children.

In child protection work the degree of confidentiality will be governed by the need to protect the child. Social workers and others working with a child and family must make clear to those providing information that confidentiality may not be maintained if the withholding of information will prejudice the welfare of the child.

(Home Office, Department of Health, Department of Education and Science, Welsh Office, 1991)

Most of the information which will be shared amongst professionals meeting the needs of children and young people with special educational needs will not fall into this category, but the principle of being able to share information for the good of the child remains the same.

The Warnock Report (DES, 1978) gives advice in this area. Paragraph 6.10 uses the idea of 'extended confidentiality' to describe the way in which multi-disciplinary teams can share information which remains 'confidential to the group' but ensures understanding of the situation by everyone. It can be very difficult to achieve this state of sharing after years of protecting professional barriers and guarding expertise (Fish, 1985). Many team members feel vulnerable, especially if their work load means that they are members of many different teams. They can feel they are leaving valuable information in all corners of the locality.

A good system of communication

In general, a good system of communication is the key to an efficient collaborative team. Team members should feel that they can talk about how they are feeling, what they wish to achieve for the child and how they hope to reach identified goals. In a team that offers support and mutual trust, members will be able to talk openly with the understanding that colleagues are actively listening. Effective communication can only be achieved if there is an openness and agreed system for recording and circulating information. This is particularly hard when team members are peripatetic staff and it often necessitates a formal mode of communication, such as regular team meetings and the passing round of an information notebook as well as the more informal chats in the corridor and at lunch times.

As effective communication is so vital to the working of effective teams, this subject will be discussed at greater length in a later section of this chapter.

Clear agreed objectives

Collaborative working will only be successful if everyone in the team has a commitment to the goals and objectives agreed by all members. The combined purpose and importance of the team's work should be fully understood by all. This sounds very difficult to achieve when different disciplines or specialisms are involved. If you ask a subject teacher and a support teacher for their aims and objectives with a particular pupil, you find their answers differ considerably. Sometimes compromise is necessary and sometimes one teacher must see the other's point of view and frequently they must agree on goals which are quite different from their original ideas. But, in the end, if the two do not agree, the pupil will be pulled in two different directions and achieve very little.

Utilisation of members' resources

Each member will bring different abilities, skills, knowledge and experience to the team. A good team will consist of members who complement each other. Individual expertise will be recognised with an understanding by each member of the contribution being made by all to the identified objectives. Parents have often had token membership to multi-disciplinary teams as the information they have offered about their child has been perceived as anecdotal and of little relevance to that gained by specialist personnel during formal assessment procedures. Now, with the recognition of 'parents as partners', the value of information they hold can be recognised.

A supportive environment (external)

There must exist a means of organisation which enables members to achieve their common purpose. There must be a comfortable place where teams can meet and discuss without constant interruptions, there should be facilities which can be used by each member and there should be back-up support of secretarial time.

The physical location of a team may have an influence upon how it works. If the collaborative team always meets at the home of the child, the family may feel invaded. The team members may not feel comfortable and the meetings will not be productive. If the meetings are held in a room which has constant interruptions, such as a telephone ringing, then the team will become distracted and the goals will not be achieved. Special needs teams which are based on the same site have a much better chance of working effectively. Meetings are easier to arrange, informal discussions can be snatched at convenient moments and team members feel that they can really get to know their colleagues.

One of the greatest problems faced by teams which span different disciplines and/or specialisms and who do not share a site, is finding time within a busy schedule to be able to work alongside each other. If collaborative work is to be achieved, managers must recognise the need to provide time for teams to meet and plan and work together. In small special schools, this can be hard to achieve but the increased quality of work can more than compensate for the time taken. In most situations, if teamwork is valued, time can be provided to ensure it happens.

Forming a collaborative team

There have been numerous studies of group processes (Woodcock, 1979; Zander, 1982; Payne, 1982; Trethowan, 1985). One of most well known is the work of Tuckman (1965) who identified four stages of group dynamics namely, 'forming', 'storming', 'norming' and 'performing'. He suggests that most groups go through these stages and a brief summary of his ideas will contribute towards a greater understanding of the ways in which teams work.

Forming
At this initial stage the group is not a team but a number of individuals with a common interest (in this case a child with special needs). During this stage the purpose of the group/team is discussed along with the identification of possible roles and the projected involvement and life span. It is in the forming period that individuals are keen to establish themselves. They check whether they belong to the group and what they might achieve.

Storming
This is the stage where there is competition for position. It may be overt or covert and is not always easy to recognise. It can be an uncomfortable time for the group as the purposes, roles, leadership and personal norms may be challenged. If people enter the team with a personal agenda it is usually during the storming stage that this is revealed. Interpersonal conflicts may become apparent but with the correct leadership these can be channelled and the formation of the vital ingredient, trust, can take place. This is a crucial stage in which members come to terms with each other, understand each other's roles and personalities. If it is not experienced, then there will be a lack of 'togetherness' which will prevent effective working at a later stage.

150

Norming

During this stage the team establishes ways of working and the normal procedures under which it can work. Individuals take responsibilities for roles and there is usually a lot of cautious experimentation by some members as they find out what they can and cannot do within the confines of the team.

Performing

Although there will have been some kind of performance before this stage, it is only when the three previous stages have been experienced that the team can be fully productive in meeting the needs of the child and family. At this stage members of the group are co-operating with one another to achieve the identified goals of the group and to provide support to meet one another's needs. This is the most effective time of a team's life. It can be the point where team members care, help and inform each other; plan, imagine and challenge; carry out plans and implement solutions; celebrate, reflect or review (Mulligan, 1988).

Where there is a common aim and a clearly defined task which is regarded by all team members as being extremely important, as with the child in need, then the forming, storming and norming processes of development may take place during the first meeting and will not be as time consuming as research has found in industrial settings (Hogg, 1990).

Team development

In management training in industry there is much interest in 'team building' to enable development, where people who normally work together are taken out of their work situation to concentrate on building themselves into a more efficient team. Exercises can vary from problem solving in the 'great outdoors' to discussion of real problems and relationships relevant to current organisational objectives. Much of the team building activity entails the risk of some personal discomfiture and teams gain strength from sharing experiences (Brian, 1992).

This kind of team building is often not possible nor perhaps even desirable in special education, but team development can sometimes be in need of help. Occasionally an outside consultant or facilitator can be useful, but often teams can direct this themselves by conducting a team review or audit. There are several publications which can help teams to review their progress by printing lists of questions to ask or by directing thinking in a specific way (Woodcock and Francis, 1981; Rowntree, 1989; Payne, 1982; Dyer, 1977).

The next chapter will contain a more extensive discussion concerning team building, review and evaluation when the subject will be 'Training Issues'. For the moment, we will move on to consider the importance of team leaders and understanding general issues concerning leadership.

Leadership

Early studies of leadership contained discussion of whether effective leaders were blessed with particular traits or used particular consistent patterns of behaviour that made them successful. Much has been made of leadership styles and a favoured typology identifies three:

- *autocratic* leaders who dictate to their followers without consultation
- *democratic* leaders involve their followers in decision making
- *laissez-faire* leaders abdicate and participate in decision making on the same level as their followers

(Guirdham, 1990, p.363)

Others suggest a slightly different set of styles and Trethowan (1985) has summarised these.

- Authoritarian style (tell them)
- Persuasive style (sell it to them)
- Participative style (share it with them)
- Delegating style (trust them to get on with it)

Research has demonstrated that there is no one style which is most effective for all situations, and the best leaders know when to employ which approach. Situational leaders are influenced by certain factors.

- the clarity of the group's task
- the quality of the relationship between the leader and the followers
- the amount of power held by the leader
- the maturity or experience of the followers or group members

Fig 6.1, reproduced from Hersey and Blanchard (1982), illustrates how style can vary according to the combination of the factors and indicates just how complex it can become.

Figure 6.1   Variations of Style

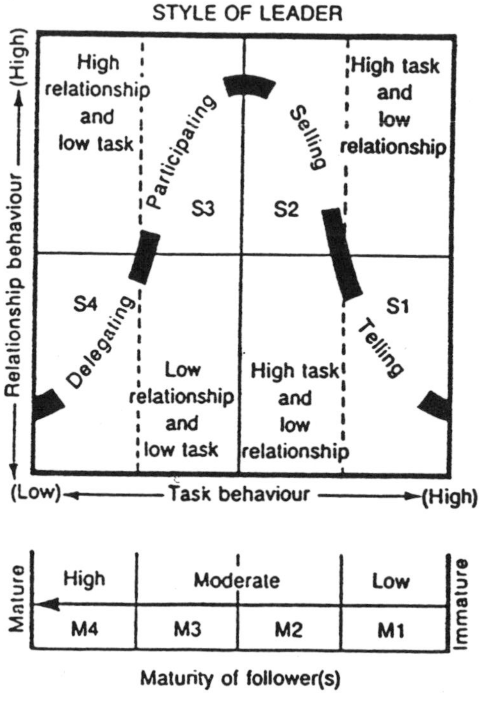

STYLE OF LEADER

(Low) ◄─────── Task behaviour ───────► (High)

High	Moderate		Low
M4	M3	M2	M1

Mature ◄─────────────────────► Immature

Maturity of follower(s)

Source: Hersey and Blanchard, 1982, p.152.

Although this is very interesting and can enable us to understand a little more about leadership in the abstract, we need to turn now to more practical matters to help potential team leaders to function effectively.

We will return briefly to Halpin's 'open climate' (in Hoyle, 1988) and consider the dimensions related to leaders that make it work; a strong commitment to leading by the example of hard work, consideration of the needs of others and working closely with the rest of the team. Adair (1984) has a useful list of key leadership functions which provide some guidance for team leaders on how to conduct themselves effectively.

Planning
- seeking all available information
- defining group task, purpose or goal
- making workable plans

Initiating
- briefing group on the aims and the plan
- explaining why aim or plan is necessary
- allocating tasks to group members
- setting group standards

Controlling
- maintaining group standards
- influencing tempo
- ensuring all actions are taken towards objectives
- keeping discussion relevant
- prodding group to action/decision

Supporting
- expressing acceptance of persons and their contributions
- encouraging group/individuals
- disciplining group/individuals
- creating team spirit
- relieving tension with humour
- reconciling disagreements or getting others to explore them

Informing
- clarifying task and plan
- giving new information to the group i.e. keeping them in the picture
- receiving information from the group
- summarising suggestions and ideas coherently

Evaluating
- checking feasibility of an idea
- testing consequences of a proposed solution
- evaluating group performance
- helping the group to evaluate its own performance against standards

(Adair, 1984, p.13)

This is a long and comprehensive list and could be very daunting for some of the teams that are formed in special education, especially when there is no recognised leader within the group. Often teams are made up of individuals who do not hold any specific status over each other. Who should take on the role of leader? Is it necessary to have one leader? Can the role be shared?

Co-ordinators of teams

Evans *et al.* (1989) point to four different levels of collaboration needed for the 'triangle of services' in special education to function most effectively; mandate (elected members of Local Authorities), strategic (directors of services), operational (heads of support services and advisers) and fieldworker (individual professionals). Usually at the levels of mandate, strategic or operational working there is a natural hierarchy which helps an appropriate leader to emerge, but often at the fieldworker level there must be some consensus concerning co-ordination of the team's work. However it is decided, there is a need for someone to bring together the work of the team. Someone must be responsible for calling meetings, running them, monitoring decisions, writing up the results and ensuring action has been taken. This role may alternate between team members according to the identified agenda. In special education this often falls to the class teacher, who has an overall picture of the child's needs. In a few schools, there is recognition that there needs to be a key member of staff in a co-ordinating position.

> Example
> In a school for pupils with physical disabilities, one member of staff has a post of responsibility for multi-disciplinary teamwork throughout the school. She is a member of the senior management team and holds some power for decision making. This does not prevent individual class teachers from being co-ordinators of the their own particular team and, in fact, teachers are encouraged to be responsible for their own liaison with therapists and specialists. There is a mechanism for annual meetings and encouragement for professionals to work alongside each other in the classroom and specialist rooms.

Communication

Whether the team is led by a true leader or facilitated by a co-ordinator, developing effective communication is the key to success in any situation where two or more human beings are interacting. Good communication skills are required when ideas and experiences are shared; when you want to find out more about something and when you are explaining what you want. Learning to communicate effectively can enhance general coping skills and overall efficiency. A specialist social worker once stated that he saw his main aim when working with parents as developing their communication skills in order to help them express their needs, hopes, fears and desires for their child. In order to be part of the collaborative team, all members should develop ways of communicating, through language and non-verbal body signals (such as leaning forward to indicate interest).

Communication is a two-way process. To be a good communicator one has to be an active listener in addition to a clear, coherent speaker. Those people who are seen as good communicators:

- generally know what they want to say;
- gain the attention of the listener/s;
- choose when and where to communicate;
- ask for clarification of messages they do not fully understand;
- respond to verbal and non-verbal feedback during interaction;
- do not become distracted during a conversation or meeting;
- know how to close a conversation or communication;
- are genuinely interested in listeners, their lives and what they have to contribute.

With skilful communication techniques, one is able to establish and maintain worthwhile working relationships.

Mulligan (1988) suggests there are eight strategies for effective communication and we will use his headings in relation to communicating in collaborative teams in special education.

1. Preparing the message

When communicating within a collaborative team, it is necessary to know exactly what you wish to communicate and achieve. Your objective should be presented in a clear, coherent manner with the main aim stated early in the process. Think in terms of a simple checklist with the following kinds of questions:

What do I want to say and achieve?
Who do I say it to?

How shall I communicate my message?
When and where will be the best time and place?
Will my message be clear to all members of the team?
Are the facts I am presenting correct?
Is there enough information?

2. Preparing yourself

It is essential that before entering into a form of communication you are fully prepared with relevant information at your fingertips. In this way you will feel more confident and consequently develop a positive image within the team. Getting to a meeting in good time by organising your diary and allowing enough time to gather papers will all influence how you communicate. Sitting stressed in a traffic jam and arriving late without the minutes of the last meeting or without the appropriate information required by the team is a recipe for disaster as far as communication is concerned and all the wrong messages will be given to other members of the team.

3. Gaining attention

Within a supportive atmosphere each member of the collaborative team should be able to expect attention when they have something to communicate. An effective communicator should possess the skills to gain attention by directly asking for it, by eye contact, by body gestures and by positioning within the group or with the listener.

4. Preparing the receiver/s

Many of the points covered in collaborative meetings may not be what some members want to hear. For example there may be additional work required, there may not be the finances available for equipment required, or problems may have multiplied since the last meeting. It is necessary in these circumstances to prepare the listeners for the importance of the communication and to ensure clarity of the information.

5. Sending the message

A collaborative team will consist of members from different disciplines, each with their own unique language and jargon. When in the process of communicating within the team, it is essential that simple jargon-free language is used. The main point of the message must not be lost in too much detail and irrelevant information. There is nothing to be gained by 'blinding colleagues with science', in fact the specialists who command the most respect are the ones who can explain their knowledge in clear terms which dissolve the mystique associated with many areas of health, education and social services.

When speaking, it is important to remember to speak clearly, at a pace which is not so slow that people are lulled into sleep nor so quickly that major points are unheard. Vary the pitch, tone and volume of your voice so that you maintain interest and attention. Convey your own interest, commitment and belief in what you are saying and talk to people not at them. Seat yourself so that you can gain eye contact with everyone and look at them each in turn to see if your message has been understood.

6. Receiving and clarifying

Active listening is not a skill which comes easily to many people, especially some professionals who, for the majority of their working day, are in a position where others listen to them. Listening is not a matter of being quiet while a person is speaking. Listening is an active process of attending to what is being said by the speaker. During collaborative team meetings it is essential that members 'follow and support' each speaker, i.e. allowing enough time for the whole of what a speaker has to say without interrupting and offer encouragers if there are problems of articulation or, as in some cases, emotions cause difficulties with recalling information. The team needs to feel confident with silences which can be necessary for the speaker to gather their thoughts and feelings. Body language which tells the speaker that you are embarrassed or not interested can cause unease and vital information may not be shared with the team.

During communications, beware of becoming distracted because you disagree with what is being said, or because you are preoccupied with a different problem (support staff who are members of several different teams may find that the issues being discussed in one situation are not as pressing as those with another child, and therefore may find it difficult concentrating on what is being said).

Active listening cannot be achieved if you fall into the trap of getting hooked on minor details. Many main points have been missed by individuals concentrating on trivia. During the 'forming' and 'storming' stages of team development active listening may not occur if members are trying to win points over other members.

Team building exercises concentrate upon active listening, which is a skill which requires careful consideration if members are to become 'good communicators'.

7. Closing a conversation/meeting

Often meetings (and conversations) can become boring, stuck at a particular point, destructive, or it may have achieved its purpose and members have gone off at tangents. At such times it is essential that the meeting (conversation) is closed. Strategies which are employed by an effective communicator (and should be used by a skilled chairperson) are:

- summarising what has been said/achieved
- suggest ways forward and future action
- thank the person/people for their time
- arrange another meeting

The team leader/co-ordinator should possess the skills to ensure that meetings have an agenda with a set time. Efficient chairpersons keep aware of the time and make sure that meetings start and finish at the stated times.

The whole issue of arranging and organising meetings is one which must be included in the training of leaders and co-ordinators. With so much valuable and expensive time spent in meetings, efficiently organised meetings are a must.

8. Following up

Once a meeting/communication has taken place, there needs to be follow up action which may take the form of a written summary of decisions made and action to be carried out along with the date of any future meeting. The written documentation should be sent to all parties involved with the child and family, especially those members of the collaborative team who may be affected by the outcome, who have to take action or who need to be aware for information.

Effective communication skills must be developed within the collaborative team because each member of the team is an individual with very different needs, interests, goals and ways of perceiving the world and therefore the sender and receiver of a message may each put entirely different interpretations upon a piece of information. Possessing good communication skills can enable a person to be an active member of the team, whereas poor communication skills can often result in isolation, confusion, frustration and resentment towards other members. As we saw earlier, effective communication is helped by the development of an open, supportive atmosphere within the team where there is mutual respect for individual skills, views and feelings, even if these are in direct opposition to those of others.

Support and self esteem

Once a supportive atmosphere has been created within a team, members are more willing to give and take feedback without causing or taking offence. There is a willingness to talk more openly about themselves and their feelings. Many parents and professionals who are not regularly part of a collaborative team, need to feel that the atmosphere is one of support before they will share their views. This process may take time and several meetings as the team travels through the stages outlined earlier in this chapter.

During team development it is essential that the 'I'm OK, You're OK' stage is reached by each team member so that there is mutual respect and everyone realises that they will not necessarily be liked by everyone else but that this does not mean that they are not respected (Harris, 1970).

A major factor that affects our ability to communicate is our self esteem. If we do not value ourselves or what we have to say then we will not view it as worthwhile to contribute to meetings. People who possess a positive self concept have feelings of confidence and self worth, can express their feelings, handle negative feedback and manage conflict. It can, however, be very difficult to raise self esteem in times of difficulty caused by understaffing, under-resourcing, restructuring or threat of closure. Parents may find it particularly difficult to maintain feelings of self worth, especially as they may well have a mixture of negative feelings such as those identified by Losen and Losen (1985), passivity, anxiety, dependency, guilt, mistrust, a fear of labelling, and a lack of full awareness of their child's difficulties. In these circumstances the collaborative team needs to provide additional support and create a non threatening atmosphere which provides positive feedback.

Communicating in team meetings

Team meetings are a central aspect of teamwork. Finding time to meet together is always difficult, but well run meetings can save an enormous amount of time which would otherwise be spent in individual exchange of information or 'finding out for oneself'. It has already been indicated that senior managers are responsible for ensuring that the time is found for regular team meetings. Some support teams have solved the problem of finding time by only functioning in schools on four days a week, keeping the fifth day for administration and meetings.

Time can be made for the specialist team to meet but this does not so often happen for the team in school which could span different specialisms and disciplines. A weekly meeting in school would probably be unnecessary, but a termly planning meeting is the very least that should happen. Ideally, there should also be a separate evaluation meeting at the end of term to feed the planning meeting at the beginning of the next.

Circumstances are different in each school and the frequency of meetings will be a matter for the particular teams involved. If the team consists of just two people as it might in a secondary school, the subject teacher and the support teacher, organising meetings is a relatively simple affair. There will be a need for the minimum of formality although there will still be a need for goals and objectives, recommendations written up and distributed to interested parties.

Many people's hearts sink when meetings are mentioned. They have experienced hours of frustration through wasted time, lack of purpose or commitment, poor follow-through, the domination of a few members and hidden agendas. Meetings are difficult to run well and very few people have had any training to help them perform better. Even people who are not in senior management posts will be likely to run meetings at some point, and in fact a truly collaborative team will rotate the role of chairperson.

Things people like about meetings

- Clear role definition of the membership − what the team and its members are supposed to do.
- Careful time control. Starting on time and ending on time. Enough time to get the work done and no more.
- Team members who are sensitive to each other's needs and

expressions; people who listen and respect each other's opinions.

- An informal relaxed atmosphere, rather than a formal exchange.
- Good preparation on the part of the chairperson and team members. Materials prepared and provided.
- Members who are all qualified and interested. They want to be part of the team. A definite commitment exists.
- Interruptions that are avoided or kept to the minimum.
- Good minutes or records are kept, so that decisions are not lost. There is no need to search out what decisions were made.
- Periodically, the team stops and assesses its own performance. Needed improvements are worked out.
- Team members feel they are given some kind of reward for their team efforts. Recognition and appreciation are given, so that they feel they are really making a contribution.
- The work of the team is accepted and used, and seems to make a contribution to the work with pupils with special needs.

(adapted from Dyer, 1977, pp.75–6)

Although there are classically three purposes for team meetings:

- to communicate information
- to solve problems
- to make decisions

in fact this is only the tip of the iceberg. Hastings *et al.* (1986) suggest that there are several other purposes.

- creating identity, cohesion and togetherness by making the team visible and giving individuals support
- producing involvement, ownership and commitment through everyone being involved
- developing synergy by sparking ideas off each other and producing 'a whole which is greater than the sum of its parts'
- reinforcing the team's ground rules by seeing them in action
- celebrating success through sharing results

(Hastings *et al.*, 1986, pp.106–7)

These authors go on to provide a very useful 'Ten Golden Rules for successfully working together' and although they were writing about industry, we find no difficulty in relating these to teams working in special education.

1. Preparation

An agenda and relevant papers should have been circulated sufficiently in advance to enable team members to read and prepare themselves. They should bring any relevant material with them and even perhaps meet with any significant others to help the meeting be as productive as possible.

2. Purpose

Everyone should be clear about what they want to get out of the meeting. Sometimes this is clear from the agenda but sometimes it is necessary to place individual objectives on the table before the meeting begins. This is particularly so if the meeting has been convened spontaneously.

3. Time scheduling

After deciding upon a 'guillotine time', contributions to the debate should be characterised by their brevity and pithiness. Sometimes it is necessary to pursue something in more detail than was planned. If this happens then a rescheduling of agenda items may be necessary or the expanded item may need to be awarded a separate meeting.

4. Creating understanding

There are three very useful interpersonal skills which help communication to be clear in meetings. *Active listening* will enable appropriate responses and the development of ideas. *Asking for clarification* will clear up misunderstandings and is particularly useful in teams where different disciplines are represented. *Summarising* helps to keep the team on task and the objectives in mind.

5. Staying on track

This can be difficult to achieve especially if team members have favourite 'hobby horses' and dominate the discussion with them. The chairperson needs to keep a firm hand and push the debate towards conclusions or decisions.

6. Using diverse experience and skills

An effective team makes good use of the qualities, skills and expertise of its members. In meetings there must be an open and supportive atmosphere where everyone feels able to contribute and be listened to. This does not mean that there will be no disagreement, but that any diversity of viewpoint will be constructive rather than destructive.

7. The creative problem solving approach

It is a good idea to try to record information and ideas as they are thrown into the arena. Flip charts are useful for this. Sometimes suggestions get lost in the heat of the discussion and the chance to develop these can be forgotten. During the exchanges, it is very useful to have a team member who keeps coming back to an idea with questions such as 'what if' or 'could we'. Often this can result in more creative problem solving.

8. Checking for agreement

Although there can rarely be complete agreement amongst members, especially if the team includes some inventive thinkers, there must be some decisions made as a result of the meeting. Conflict in effective teams can be extremely useful (and there is a section in this chapter set aside for this). It can provide energy, prevent complacency and even produce the best ideas. However, there must be some kind of resolution if the team is to move forward and ratify future action on the part of its members.

9. Review the working of the team

Time should be spent on brief feedback concerning how well the meeting went. Effective teams are never satisfied and are continually looking for ways in which to improve their performance, particularly at meetings. There may be a need to set aside time in a specific meeting at the end of the year to review progress in more detail.

10. Action

Following decisions made, there must be some kind of action. Minutes of the meeting should be circulated as soon as possible, and on this there should be clear indications about who agreed to do what. It is no good sending out minutes with the agenda for the next meeting as most of the action should have been done by then.

Practical considerations

The final things to consider about running effective meetings include some advice about practical considerations:

- ensure the meeting room is comfortable with a table which enables all members to see each other;
- have flip charts or an overhead projector available;
- put the phone through to someone else;
- make sure the room is not too hot and provide drinks;
- use techniques such as brainstorming or breaking into smaller groups for discussion if the momentum flags;
- invite outsiders to a meeting if a fresh viewpoint is needed or if that person is a 'gatekeeper' for what you wish to do;
- if possible, maintain the same time and meeting place so that a team identity is encouraged. If it is necessary to vary meeting places, perhaps have a reliable rota so everyone knows where the next meeting will be and when;
- hold short frequent meetings rather than infrequent long ones. Again, if this is not possible, try to ensure informal conversations between members to keep the flow of communication;
- when the team does meet they will probably need some time to catch up on gossip, so build that into the schedule. This exchange is actually very important for team members to feel their way into the team again.

Handling conflict

Conflict has been mentioned several times during this book and many writers have useful things to say about making conflict into something positive in collaborative teams (Easen, 1985; Dyer, 1977; Payne, 1982; Guirdham, 1990).

Irving Janis' term 'Groupthink' is a good reminder for us all that it is not necessarily a good thing always to be in agreement with each other. The symptoms of 'Groupthink' include:

- an illusion of invulnerability;
- discounting of warnings;
- an unquestioned belief in the group's inherent morality;
- stereotyped views of rivals;
- direct pressure on those who disagree;
- self-censorship of deviations from the apparent group consensus;
- a shared illusion of unanimity;
- the emergence of people who protect the group from adverse information.

(Easen, 1985, pp.18–19)

However, badly handled conflict can be as much of a problem as this 'Groupthink'. Conflict can be defined as 'the tension between two or more social entities (individuals, groups or larger organisations) which arises from the incompatibility of actual or desired responses' (Raven and Kruglanski, 1970 in Guirdham, 1990). From this statement the importance of communication in the process is indicated, which in its turn points to the way in which many teams handle conflict. Most team building exercises expect members to confront conflict and work through it to find a solution of some kind.

There are times when this exercise is just too difficult. When real conflicts of interest exist there may be a complete breakdown of relationships between people. In this case, bringing every issue out into the open may destroy any hope of resolving the situation. There are ways of bringing conflict to an end and limiting the damage caused and Payne (1982) suggests they fall into two basic strategies; *control strategies* which can prevent conflict from flaring up or enable things to be held steady while *confrontation* is employed to try to resolve it.

Control strategies

- avoidance of situations where disputes arise;
- alteration of the form or place of the conflict;
- feedback to the parties involved about how their conflict is affecting others;

166

- support for the consequences of conflict with more rest and thinking time.

Confrontation

This should be carefully planned:

- both parties must want to resolve the situation;
- both parties must be on equal footing during the confrontation (difference in status must be ignored);
- first overtures should be in an enquiry mode and responses should be equally positive;
- both parties describe the situation as they see/understand it and they discuss the similarities between them, acknowledging common goals and mutual respect and finding positive actions they can share.

Outside consultants or facilitators can help the situation by promoting the idea that openness is acceptable and that resolution is expected.

Negotiation

An important skill in the arena of conflict is that of negotiation. One of the tricks of successful negotiation is for both parties to feel that they have done well. If it is allowed to degenerate into a slanging match then no agreement is likely. The eventual outcome should be a win-win situation where everyone is satisfied rather than a win-lose situation where someone feels aggrieved. It is not always possible for this to happen, so it may be necessary for there to be a compromise and the party who loses most may have to be placated with some kind of 'compensation'. This may involve a shift of workload or a change of work mates etc.

Forsyth (1991) suggests ten techniques to help manage negotiation. We summarise these below:

- use silence – sometimes this is more valuable than giving your view;
- summarise frequently – especially if negotiations are complex;
- take notes – this can give you time to clarify things;
- leave the other party feeling that each step is good – build the negotiation up bit by bit;
- read between the lines – remember that negotiation has an

adversarial element and often the other party is playing an inner game;

- maintain neutrality as much as possible — negotiation is a balancing act;
- keep thinking — sometimes you will need to make time like making a phone call or making more notes;
- keep your powder dry — don't finalise things until you are sure you have all the facts;
- don't get hung up on deadlines — remember they are negotiable too;
- constraints and variables are interchangeable — even so-called fixed things can be made negotiable.

(Forsyth, 1991, pp.29–32)

Once again, the business flavour of this kind of list can be discerned, but anyone trying to negotiate with a colleague from a different discipline or specialism in special education will recognise the need for the kind of advice offered in this extract. With funding under Local Management of Schools becoming so disparate, more negotiation will be expected of more people. Forming contracts between support services and schools will become more and more necessary and individuals will be looking for training in this area. This subject will come up again in the chapter concerning training issues.

Working together

The final section in this chapter is concerned with the way in which special education teams actually work together. We have spent much time exploring how teams can become truly collaborative and how things can go wrong. It is now time to turn to what team members actually do together.

Problem solving

Solving problems in teams is different from individual problem solving. Team members have to commit themselves to the solution even if it is not exactly that at which they would have arrived themselves. The advantage is that solutions arrived at by teams can be said to have a broader base of support and the work involved in a difficult task can be spread over the complementary skills of several individuals (Payne, 1982).

A much neglected part of problem solving is actually defining the problem in the first place. A 'force-field' analysis can be a useful way to begin. This involves listing all the restraining forces and positive forces and weighing the two up against each other and it comes from the work of Kurt Lewin's field theory (Payne, 1982).

Figure 6.2   Force-field Analysis

Restraining Forces

Positive Forces

Another possibility is to use a SWOT analysis where the following keywords are used as triggers to identify the reality of situations.

Strengths
Weaknesses
Opportunities
Threats

Lists that are made under these subtitles can be very powerful yet this is a simple way to analyse the problem and move towards a solution.

A simple phase model of problem solving is suggested by Guirdham (1990, p.340).

Phase 1   Recognise problems and diagnose characteristics
Phase 2   Develop ideas and obtain information
Phase 3   Evaluate alternatives and select one for implementation

In many real situations, team members have to move backwards and forwards through these phases, but some kind of logical procedure seems to bring the most consistent problem solving.

The generation of creative solutions can be very productive in teams, as long as controversy does not generate into conflict. A useful technique is 'brainstorming' where ideas are fired rapidly at a scribe who records them on a flip chart with no comment or criticism. Unusual and controversial thoughts are encouraged and are eventually given due consideration, perhaps through the 'field-force' or 'SWOT' analyses.

Decision making

In many cases, in collaborative teams, decisions will have been arrived at through a problem solving technique, but there are other occasions when either the leader/co-ordinator or individuals will make decisions alone.

One blockage to the effective functioning of teams can be the fact that decision making procedures have never been discussed and understood by members. Sometimes there is no need for intricate discussion and decisions are made by the person for whom it holds the greatest interest but if the effect will be felt by all members then discussion is not only necessary but vital.

Trethowan (1985, p.16) suggests the following stages of team decision making:

Stage 1 awareness of the decision situation (why do we need a decision? what is the nature of the problem?)

Stage 2 analysis of the alternative solutions and the merits and demerits of these (what choices do we have?)

Stage 3 selecting and implementing the decision, telling or selling it to others if necessary to ensure success (this is what we do)

Stage 4 collecting feedback and reviewing the decision to evaluate whether it achieved its purpose (did it work? if not, why not?)

And don't forget that a decision is only as good as its implementation! No matter how brilliant the decision, it will be ruined by being carried out half-heartedly or by only a few members of the team. This particular situation has been seen so many times in special education and the children are always the losers. If everyone is tackling problems in the same way, there is much more likelihood of progress for individual pupils.

All this advice is very simple and seems as if we are stating the obvious but it is not very often that special education teams consider the mechanics of the ways in which they need to work in order to be most effective. It is very easy to get swept away with the stressful business of large case loads and unco-operative colleagues that simple solutions fade into insignificance.

Reviewing teams

This really brings the whole cycle back to the beginning and concludes this examination on working together collaboratively.

Feedback to team members should include a review of all the things which help to make it effective or ineffective as well as the more tangible achievements such as data concerning pupil progress. Both types of information are useful and will help to evaluate the work of the team as a whole as well as the contributions by individual members.

Payne (1982, pp.28–9) makes some useful suggestions for criteria for assessing teams and the ways in which they work:

Goals and how they are agreed
Internal and external expectations of the team
Leadership and how it is organised
Communication and group processes describing how the team works
Value systems and norms that exist among members
How decisions are made
Self-development and regular review of work
Physical environment

These are very often the forgotten parts of review and it is essential for collaborative teams to spend some time regularly in considering these areas as the more the members understand about the way in which their team works, the greater the possibility for effectiveness.

One of the other forgotten things is that few members of special education teams have any training in this aspect of their work and in the next chapter, we examine training opportunities and the content of courses specifically run for teams of professionals drawn from different specialisms or disciplines.

CHAPTER 7

Training for Collaboration

Management training in special educational needs

All through this book we have been concerned with aspects of management in special education. Training in this area is relatively new, in fact any training in education management for practising teachers has only recently become available and much of that is aimed only at headteachers (Freeman and Gray, 1989). There is very little for those who work in the classroom, which demonstrates how little we recognise that management issues are important for all professionals, particularly as organisations are generally moving towards a more democratic way of working and everyone is expected to contribute to organisation development in some way.

A consideration of courses on management run by LEAs or Institutes of Higher Education shows very little take-up by senior staff concerned with special needs in mainstream and special schools (Salmon, 1987). The content of such courses appear to have little specific reference to SENs which would perhaps explain the lack of appeal to those working in special education. There are, of course, many issues in management that are relevant to all types of schools and HMI, quite rightly, recommend that there should not really be any division into special and mainstream for training in these areas (Salmon, 1987).

Although we are not suggesting that management training in general should be separate for special educators, there are times when the emphasis is different and training should enable course participants to focus specifically on the parts that are most relevant for their work. For example, it could be argued that working with parents can be more demanding in special education which would indicate the need for more intensive training in this area. Likewise, legislation is specialised and calls for a deeper understanding from those who work with it constantly. Working in the collaborative manner expounded in this book is another example of the need for specific training. We have seen, in earlier chapters, how difficult it is to achieve. In this chapter we will explore how focused training can help.

Working together with colleagues involves the development of a whole new set of skills, knowledge and understanding in support staff. McLaughlin (1989) points also to the need for staff to explore attitudes and develop interpersonal skills to help diminish the difficulties found in face-to-face work with other professionals. She feels that training is particularly needed in this area as this is where teachers often feel they lack specific expertise. Supporting or working alongside colleagues is demanding work, prone to conflict and resistance and special training is essential.

Before we move into looking at the content and methods of courses about collaboration, we would like to spend some time in consideration of the generalities of staff development and how we can manage change in the workplace. It is axiomatic that moving towards working collaboratively will involve both these aspects and a greater understanding of what is involved will increase the likelihood of subsequent training being effective.

Managing change

Affecting change in institutions is a very complex task and the study of both theory and practice can help in the formation of successful strategies for managing its implementation.

Theories of change

Several different models of change have been tried over the years. The first is concerned with the attempt to change institutions from the outside and the phrase 'research, development and diffusion' (RD & D) has been coined to describe it. The kind of curriculum development tried in the 1960s, through the Curriculum Council falls into this model, where research workers produced new materials which, after trial in pilot schools, they mass-produced for use across the country.

There are enormous problems with this model, particularly at the diffusion stage. Often change was seen to be cosmetic, leaving underlying beliefs untouched. Staff on the periphery of the change proposals can choose to ignore the directives from the centre and this is often what happened. In fact the National Curriculum can be seen to have been introduced in an RD & D manner. It is very much a centre-periphery approach but the important difference is that there is legislation to ensure that the changes do take place in the classroom. It is still difficult to change people's beliefs and values by legislation but if you know that you have got to make the new proposals work you are encouraged to consider them more carefully.

A second approach in this mode concentrates more on the dissemination part of the model. Each member of the organisation is taken through stages from awareness to adoption carefully and slowly. Personal contact and communication are seen as of paramount importance and emphasis is on training and discussion. The receiver of the innovation is still regarded as having rather a passive role but the centre of the reform is seen as being more local or regional than central. There is usually a project team involved and it is when they have withdrawn that many innovations have been seen to have failed or only partially succeeded. Cascade training can be seen to fall into this mode, where one person is trained for example as a special needs co-ordinator and he or she in turn trains staff at school. The training may or may not have an effect in the classroom, it rather depends on how necessary the change is perceived by individual members of staff.

A third model in this mode is called a problem solving approach. The institution and its problems are at the centre of the stage and help from outside is sought in the form of a consultancy which yields ideas to be adapted to individual circumstances. Even though this model is looking more closely at the needs of the institution there is still an emphasis on the system rather than the individuals as the focus of the change.

All these approaches have a common view of the world of organisations where individuals are treated in terms of the roles that they play within the institution rather than their particular personal needs. There is another view of change which adopts a different standpoint and it is related to a set of theories called phenomenology. Writers in this camp place individuals and their view of the world at the centre of the discussion. The word 'micro-politics' has been coined to describe this view of institutions. Central issues are identified as power and control and the way in which individuals exert these over each other. Innovation is seen in terms

174

of the group and members' relationships to each other. Understanding this layer of organisational life can help us to see why change is so difficult to affect, but on its own, this theory is of little more help for extracting practical help for implementing change than those described above.

As with most theories professionals working in organisations need an eclectic approach so that each idea can inform their future practice. It is important to combine the knowledge that change imposed from outside (RD & D) is difficult to implement and that individual relationships are a very important dimension. Working through the problems presented by theory can help inform practice. Of course, the obverse is also true as practice can undoubtedly inform theory.

Resistance to change

Before we look at how to implement successful change, it will be useful to spend some time making a list of circumstances in which, in practice, we can expect an increase in resistance to proposed change. We are sure that you will recognise some or all of these.

- you don't see the need to change;
- you have not been given a clear reason by anyone else;
- you haven't been involved in the decision making;
- information has not been communicated properly;
- it has been imposed too quickly;
- it's not part of general development;
- you have picked up mixed messages from management;
- you don't trust their motives and feel you're being manipulated;
- timetables and resources are seen as inadequate;
- all your other experiences of change have been unsuccessful;
- your hard-fought-for traditions are threatened;
- existing relationships are threatened;
- you feel deskilled and lacking in confidence;
- your feelings have been ignored;
- you aren't offered any incentives or recompense;
- you've got far too much to do anyway.

Amongst all these difficulties, it must not be thought that change is not desirable. Without change the education system would stagnate. It is so important to encourage organisations and the people who work in them to continue to grow and develop.

Successful change

Despite all the problems, many organisations do manage to implement change successfully and accounts of these can offer useful guidelines for future practice. Everard and Morris (1990) have drawn together the factors involved from three publications and we offer a summary here for your use. They used HMI (1977) *Ten Good Schools*, Peters and Waterman (1982) *In Search of Excellence* and Goldsmith and Clutterbuck *The Winning Streak*.

- The organisation has a clear sense of purpose and is goal-directed.
- The structure of the organisation is determined by work requirements and may differ for different departments. Power is dispersed according to need.
- Authority is delegated, communications are open, conflict is encouraged and collaboration is rewarded.
- Individuals are respected, work is evaluated and achievement is celebrated.
- There is an element of realism with the minimum of 'game-playing' (people are not engaged in games to build power bases or defeat rivals). There is built-in feedback and there is an action research approach to problems.
- The whole system is open and its changing demands are tracked and an appropriate response is made.
- The needs of the individual are balanced with the needs of the institution.
- There is a collegiate culture, where individuals manage to get together, there are regular opportunities for observation and discussion of each other's work.

This relates well to Halpin's 'open climate' (Hoyle, 1988) that we identified in the last chapter, the organisational climate that is most encouraging for working collaboratively.

Change in practice

Several writers have made suggestions about the best way to manage change in practice. Everard and Morris (1990) write about six stages:

1. *Diagnosis* leading to a decision about the soundness of the change programme.

2. Defining the *future state* by asking questions about what we want to happen.
3. Describing the *present* state.
4. Identifying the *gaps* between the two, who should do what and how do we manage problems.
5. Managing the *transition* between the present and the future.
6. *Evaluating and monitoring* the change.

They warn that it is not always necessary to go through each stage and that theirs is not the only approach. Whatever the approach, though, it must be systematic or time and resources will not be found for the fundamentals of training and support. Other writers point to similar practicalities and exhort innovators to look to certain areas of great importance, the need for:

- clear objectives;
- flexibility;
- participation of all involved;
- recompense for anyone who loses out;
- staff development in general.

It can be seen from this section that sudden, unprepared change delivered from on-high is unlikely to be successful. There needs to be a general climate of openness to development with the needs of staff, as part of the organisation, at the centre. Sending isolated individuals on courses and expecting them to return to change the world is not realistic and this is delightfully summed up in the following quotation.

> This then is the myth of the hero-innovator: the idea that you can produce, by training, a knight in shining armour, who, loins girded with new technology and beliefs, will assault his organisational fortress and institute changes in both himself and others at a stroke. Such a view is ingenuous. The fact of the matter is that organisations such as schools and hospitals will, like dragons, eat hero-innovators for breakfast.
>
> (Georgiades and Phillimore, in Easen, 1985, pp.162–3)

So we can see that training staff for working collaboratively and managing change is not just a matter of providing courses and hoping for the best. It is rather more complex and all-embracing than that and it is to staff development as a whole that we must now turn.

Staff development

There seem to be many activities that come under the general umbrella of staff development. Lyons and Stenning (1986) suggest:

- whole school training based on school self-review
- performance review
- mentor schemes
- team teaching
- classroom observation
- working parties/committees
- courses/research/study visits/consultancies
- job rotation
- transference between schools

Rowntree (1989) suggests a parallel set of ideas for management training in industry which is useful to consider.

- 'sitting next to Nellie'
- rotating jobs/tasks
- secondment to another section
- special assignments
- discussion groups
- guided reading
- practise under supervision
- regular direct instruction
- coaching informally

(Rowntree, 1989, p.87)

There is often difficulty with reconciling individual needs with the needs of the institution. A well-conducted staff development programme should:

1. be planned upon identified needs of the school and individuals;
2. relate to the wider development programme set up at local and national level;
3. have an agreed evaluation strategy;
4. have a procedure for reconciling conflicting claims and for encouraging staff co-operation;
5. establish priorities;
6. have clear aims and objectives.

Programmes need to be well planned and executed otherwise they will have no effect. Staff will need to feel that there is a reason for the course they are attending or the working party they are contributing to and this reason needs to be the concern of the institution as well as the individual or there will be no improvement in the teaching or learning. If there has been rigorous discussion leading to whole-school plans, there is a greater likelihood that the programme devised will meet the needs of the organisation and its staff.

Day *et al.* (1990) propose two different but related approaches to managing school development, the *functional* approach and the *developmental* approach. A combination of the two presents a picture of teachers as co-managers, 'concerned both with the tasks and activities of development policies and with the extension of their own personal and professional skills' (Day *et al.,* 1990, p.54). The system they discuss is liberated from the traditional scale-post model where a member of staff is appointed to a curriculum or management post. The tasks that need to be completed dictate the roles to be fulfilled and individual expertise or need dictates who carries them out. For example, if from discussion, mathematics and parental involvement in reading have been identified as priorities for development, then small groups may be formed in these two areas to consider the problems and present possible answers. Part of the answer may be to send a member of staff on a course, but the 'hero-innovator' syndrome can be avoided by the very fact that staff together have identified this as a need and actively want the information he or she will bring back.

Of course, working in this way creates more possibilities for teams of staff to work together, bringing all the advantages and problems identified earlier in this book. Whichever way we look there is a growing need for members of staff to be trained to work together effectively.

In-service training

As we have seen, in-service training courses are only one example of the many activities classed as staff development. They are, however, an important part and deserve consideration separately.

The recommendations of the James Report (DES, 1972) that teachers should be released with pay for one term in every seven years has not been implemented but the general call for more short courses, conferences and workshops has, on the whole, been answered (Sebba and Robson, 1988). However, much of these have been devoted to National Curriculum training since the 1988 Education Act and training for work with pupils with SENs has been somewhat submerged under the need for all staff to become familiar with the new demands.

There has been a general shift away from long courses in Institutes of Higher Education towards shorter school-focused courses which relate more closely to the needs of individual institutions and their staff. Schools are invited to assess their needs and plan courses accordingly either independently, in clusters or as part of a wider initiative.

According to ACSET, the Advisory Committee on the Supply and Education of Teachers, in-service training (INSET) should enable teachers to:

1. develop professional competence, confidence and relevant knowledge;
2. evaluate their own work and attitudes in conjunction with colleagues;
3. develop criteria with which to assess their own teaching in relation to the demands of society;
4. advance their careers;
5. monitor and shape their own professional development;
6. meet the specific needs of LEAs and schools.

(Bush *et al.*, 1980)

These are all rather ideal words, and anyone who has been part of INSET activities knows that the actual quality of courses is varied in the extreme. The best do indeed fulfil the recommendation of the ACSET but many fail to come up to this standard.

Backhouse (1987) suggests four levels of impact of training through INSET:

*   awareness;
*   formation of concepts and knowledge;
*   devising principles and gaining skills;
*   application and problem solving.

He feels that only after this is there any impact on the children's education. From this he has suggested five components of training:

1. presentation of theory/skill/strategy;
2. modelling or demonstrating these;
3. practice in simulation;

4.   feedback;
5.   coaching for application.

He has found that most successful INSET includes all five.

Course leaders need to identify desired outcomes in terms of behaviour and attitudes and then develop strategies to achieve these with course participants (Mumford, 1986, cited in West-Burnham, 1987). West-Burnham suggests a virtuous circle:

Figure 7.1   A Virtuous Circle

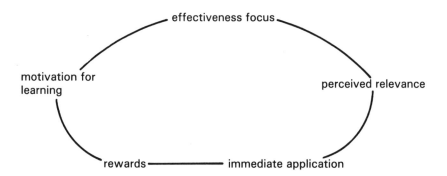

He goes on to characterise the way in which adults learn and suggests that the most appropriate learning model is experiential as it is concerned with action based on change. Process is as important as content and the outcomes are both cognitive and affective. It certainly sounds like the learning model needed to match the arguments earlier in this chapter, culminating in the recommendation that change can only really be implemented if values and attitudes change as well as skills and knowledge.

The questions that follow are a useful set to enable course providers to develop criteria to inform planning, design, implementation and evaluation.

1.   What are the desired outcomes in terms of actions and behaviour?
2.   Is the process of course delivery geared to action as well as increasing knowledge?
3.   Is the learning methodology appropriate to the intended outcomes and the needs of the participants?

4. Does the course design reflect the perceptions of both participants and their sponsors?
5. Have the potentially varying motivations of participants been explored and taken into account?
6. Is there the potential for applying the outcomes of the course in terms of time, resources and the credibility of course members?
7. Does the course planning include provisions for further development activities in response to new needs being identified?
8. Is learning in groups and are those groups designed and developed?
9. Are action methods used throughout the course?
10. Are all the tutors on the course trained to work in an experiential context?
11. What are the mechanisms for evaluation?
12. Are there appropriate mechanisms for implementing the outcomes in the course participants' institutions?
14. Is the course part of an overall development strategy in respect of long term goals based on LEA and school needs diagnosis?

(West-Burnham, 1987)

In summary we shall use a set of conditions for successful training put together by Rouse and Balshaw:

*   initial negotiation involving all staff of the school to identify development needs;
*   formulating a contract between the individual, the school, the LEA and higher education;
*   a taught element which stresses process as well as content;
*   interactive presentation;
*   projects which are likely to be of benefit to the pupils;
*   active support of the headteacher;
*   opportunities for course members to pursue their own professional development and career;
*   formative evaluation across the whole programme and summative evaluation of the project as well as the course;
*   continued post-course support for participants and their schools.

(Rouse and Balshaw, 1991, pp.99–100)

As we continue and consider the specifics of training for collaboration, there will be more discussion and practical advice concerning appropriate methods for conducting courses.

Training courses in collaboration

If we combine what we have learned about the theory and practice of staff development and the management of change, with the results of the earlier discussion concerning working in teams we should be able to begin to form ideas for suitable training courses. It will be useful to start with possible content and examples from the literature before considering the different methods available.

Course content

Although on many occasions training in collaboration will be part of other wider courses, it is possible to identify the elements needed and extract them for consideration in their own right.

- the reasons for collaboration
- the problems experienced in practice
- information about the services available
- information about each other's roles/experience/skills etc. and the constraints under which everyone works
- the dynamics of working together
- communication and other interpersonal skills
- the development of groups and teams
- team building techniques and when to use them
- working together in practice e.g.: contracts/records/observ-ation/teaching/resources/writing programmes/assessment etc.
- running effective meetings
- leadership and the role of the co-ordinator
- joint problem solving and decision making
- staff development and managing change in institutions

Fuller discussion of these elements can be found in previous chapters.

Example
A course, with collaborative work at its heart, is being developed by lecturers at the University of Birmingham in conjunction with staff associated with the British Institute of Learning Disabilities. This is a one-year part-time course for staff who work with people with profound and multiple learning disabilities (PMLD) and it includes several sessions on the theory and practice of collaboration as well as on working

with children and adults with PMLD. There are three modules each lasting for ten weeks (30 hours of teaching) and there are several layers of accreditation as the course is open to all staff who work in schools, adult centres and hospitals. Existing teams of staff are encouraged to apply to attend the course together and there is an incentive of reduced fees if this happens! Course participants who, for whatever reason, attend on their own are asked to ensure that collaborative work is possible at their place of work. If there is any difficulty anticipated then negotiations are entered into between the applicant, his or her head or manager and the course co-ordinator. It would certainly be very difficult to fulfil the practical elements of the course without the possibility of working collaboratively with colleagues.

Ideally any course involving teams of people would be run within the work place with their own work and problems as a focus for development. Extracting members and placing them in an Institute of Higher Education is not really the most efficient way of training and in an attempt to address this, a written package of the Birmingham PMLD course is being developed for staff to work through in their own situation with the help of a regional tutor. This brings its own problems of learning at a distance but hopefully the team nature of the course will help to combat feelings of isolation and difficulties with motivation.

Examples from the literature

Not many courses have been run in special education which fall into the category that we are looking for. Westhill College and Birmingham Polytechnic ran a project bringing together third year students training to be teachers of pupils with severe learning difficulties and speech therapists respectively (David and Smith, 1987; 1991). The students, in pairs, assessed a pupil with language disabilities and between them devised a language programme for use in the classroom. The aims of the project were to increase knowledge of each other's work and foster collaboration as well as increase knowledge of language assessment. Student evaluations over the five different years that the project ran, revealed that they had learned much from the experience. They were asked to suggest factors which facilitate collaboration and these were some of their replies:

184

- understanding what each has to offer
- respect for each other's expertise
- a positive attitude to teamwork and collaboration and not competition
- having an honest approach and attempting to share knowledge, not adopting an expert role
- enough time for joint consultations
- being prepared to listen and discuss
- developing a relationship of trust

(David and Smith, 1991, p.105)

This particular project has had to come to an end as there are no longer undergraduates training for special education although there are still speech therapy students at that level. There has been no attempt to pair the speech therapy students with practising teachers as it was felt that equality of level of training was important for the pairs to work well.

Another example which offers some information for training in collaboration is taken from Losen and Losen (1985). This pertains to teams already working in special education in the United States and they offer possible content for training sessions:

- exploration of role expectations;
- clarification of areas of overlap;
- development of time management and priority goal setting.

Methods are suggested which include:

- role playing;
- problem solving;
- decision making;
- peer group discussion.

Some of these suggestions will be taken up and discussed in more detail in the next section on training methods.

Training methods

There are many different sources that can help to inform the kind of training necessary for collaborative work across disciplines and specialisms. Both education and management training in industry have interesting ideas for consideration.

Robinson (1988) states that it is logical to train teams together if they are going to work together and in a business context this is often possible. It is undeniably more difficult with staff working in special education as the teams are sometimes fleeting or individuals belong to so many different teams that training with them all would be an impossibility. However, if it is possible, it is more effective to train people together as it is notoriously difficult for individuals to change the group.

The first hurdle for team training is selling it to top management (Robinson, 1988). He suggests that it is easier to get co-operation in terms of time and resources if:

- it is clear that real problems will be tackled;
- teams have the basic ability and authority to carry out projects within the training;
- target times are established and kept to;
- everyone is there *all* the time;
- team effectiveness is evaluated;
- the team is treated as a group not as individuals;
- objectives are made clear.

Within the world of management training in business, there are many different methods for working and a brief introduction to some of these will illustrate the possibilities:

- the use of case studies (the Harvard Business School method) to give 'real' exercises;
- 'action maze' case studies, where the information is deliberately limited and gradually increased as decisions are made;
- the 'incident process' where trainees are encouraged to request the missing information after scrutinising given data;
- role play, which needs to be sensitively handled and used only when team members are at ease with one another;
- simulation, which is a combination of case studies and role play (can be computerised);
- brainstorming, to stimulate creativity;
- 'fishbowl' technique, where Team A sits around Team B while they solve a problem and then offers evaluation;
- group exercises, where individuals provide solutions to problems which are then subjected to group discussion to arrive at one response;
- 'true and false' questionnaires and open questions which are then discussed;

- mini case studies focused on specific problems;
- workshops set up to tackle specific operational problems in an extension of the work situation;
- sensitivity training to increase awareness of one's own behaviour and how it is received and interpreted by others.

(Robinson, 1988, pp.114–29)

Most of these techniques are used very little in education training, the preference is for talks or lectures followed by discussion. Sometimes case studies or brainstorming are used to focus participants' thinking but very little use is made of practising problem solving and decision making, especially as part of the team with whom one is working. Using simulated situations is one of the suggestions made by Backhouse (1987) in his five components of in-service training quoted above and it is clearly relevant for training in collaborative work. Some suitable exercises will be described and discussed, beginning with those which fall into team building techniques.

Teambuilding techniques

There are various stances that can be taken concerning team-building. Some trainers use set exercises to enable team members to analyse the different roles within a team and the ways in which individuals work, while others take a much more listening and reactive role comparable to a marriage guidance counsellor. Most trainers see themselves as facilitators engaging course participants in exercises which reveal the ways in which they think and work within the team. Often one of the members is an observer of the exercise, primed to watch for certain things. The observations are then reported back and discussion ensues.

Example
This is a five-day teambuilding programme for fifteen participants with two trainers from the work of Barker (1980, p.172).
One of the exercises used by Barker during this particular course illustrates the way in which he was trying to work with participants.

Figure 7.2   Teambuilding Programme

Introductory phase	Exchange of expectations and workshop aims '3 things I like about myself' exercise.	Clarify nature and business of the week. Orientate to situation.
Self-learning phase	Learning a shared model of behaviour, using theory inputs and exercises.	Language and concepts familiarisation. Building trust in situations. Developing openness. Increasing awareness about self and others.
Self and task phases	Exercise and theory of consulting relationships.	Use of learning in relation to primary task. Bridge building to deeper levels of personal and group work.
Self and group phase	Teambuilding activities and exercises, with high emphasis on feedback and goal clarification.	Resolving interpersonal and authority conflicts. Decreasing competition, increasing mutual support and group commitment. Increasing sense of power over own destiny and influence over change processes.
Closing phase	Final exercise/s	Integrate and transfer workshop learning to organisational situation.

Group-level role negotiation
The group were asked to carry out a group-level modification of Harrison's role negotiation exercise:
    In small groups of five, list your views under the following headings:
1.   What can the group do more of or start doing?
2.   What can the group do less of or stop doing?
3.   What can the group continue to do the same of in order to maintain and increase its effectiveness?
This has a number of consequences:
1.   establishing and clarifying the group's goals;
2.   focusing the problem areas for the group, both task and interpersonal;
3.   clearing up fantasies and rumours about changes in the group;
4.   putting the in-group/out-group situation 'on the table'.

It also signalled an end to aggressive or avoiding behaviour towards the task of the workshop, and the acceptance of the staff as a resource with specific skills to contribute to that task.

(Barker, 1980, p.176)

It is possible to see from this kind of example, the way in which simple questions can be used to bring out important information about the ways in which the team is working now and how it might become more effective in the future.

Other exercises are more oblique and incidental learning emerges from what can seem as very trivial exercises, such as producing the largest number of memo pads from a given piece of paper or identifying and classifying the motor vehicles in the area (Lawn and Woods, 1988). Tasks that need to be reviewed and then re-done, reviewed and re-done highlight various group processes and the presence of a well-primed observer can be extremely useful in analysing these.

Observers

Although all members of the group engaged in a task should be aware of the things that are said and done for later discussion, one member, or sometimes two, should be nominated to sit aside in silence, simply observing. By watching carefully and making notes much that the working members missed can be helpful in the ensuing analysis. The Coverdale Organisation (1985) have produced a useful set of notes for observing members which we reproduce here.

Please remain detached from the task, and focus on the way the group is working: the teamwork rather than the technical aspects of the proceedings.

You are asked to produce facts, not to pass judgements or to say how you would have done the task.

Translate your opinions into facts by asking yourself 'What causes me to have that view? What actually happened?'

When something said or done appears important, note the consequences. Then you will be able to report objectively what happened and its effect, discarding points of little significance.

When distinct progress occurs, look for what causes it and the effect it has. If there is a difficulty, note how the group handles it.

At the end of your period as observer, prepare to rejoin the group as a working member. What will you do to help avoid any of the difficulties you saw? What will you do to promote the use of practices you saw to be of value?

(Coverdale Organisation, 1985, p.100)

Feedback that combines the data from both the observer and the working members is extremely important for the team to come to understand the ways in which they are working now and how they could work in the future. Although the exercises may be far from the usual tasks of the real job, there is no doubt that much can be learned about colleagues and about yourself in these sorts of situations.

Exercises can relate very much more directly to normal work circumstances as the following example demonstrates.

Example

A group of eighteen people who were preparing to sail round the world were taken through several days of teambuilding exercises to prepare them for the task ahead. These were a disparate set of people from all walks of life, prepared to take a year off to live in cramped conditions together. The consultant invited to train them to work together effectively mainly employed the 'marriage counsellor' manner mentioned above. He listened to their needs, set very open tasks and encouraged them to work as independently from him as they could. He also included a talk consisting of theory about hidden agendas, awareness of our pre-conscious, the importance of feedback and our perceptions of other people.

The final exercise was deliberately related to life on board ship. They were asked to work in groups of about six to compile a list of ideas for maintaining morale and good relationships during the long trip. There was a sharing of all the ideas generated and the Captain made a note of those that would need specific organisation so he could attend to the practicalities of the suggestions.

Teambuilding in special education

It is not difficult to relate all this to teambuilding with staff in special education. Most of the exercises employed in this method are content-free and can be used in many different circumstances where

190

people are trying to work together effectively. There would also need to be some exercises and discussion that focus specifically on the needs of people working within special needs, such as organising resources, agreeing on report formats and ways of working with specific pupils.

There still remains the difficulty of getting the team together to train in this way. Who is actually in the team and who is really just a member of a looser network outside the need for intensive team training? Sometimes it can be hard to tell. In the case of a group of pupils with profound and multiple disabilities, there would be great advantage in training together all those people who are in at least weekly contact. This might include the class teacher, classroom assistants, physiotherapist, occupational therapist and speech therapist. There may also be a school nurse and school social worker. These are likely to be common to a number of pupils in a class or department. Then there is the difficulty of knowing how to include parents and family social workers as, of course, each of these has only one child in common. Specific circumstances would need to dictate how this was handled.

The core team identified above would probably be much smaller in a mainstream school, but for teambuilding purposes it would be useful for the members of a subject or phase department to work together with support staff as a whole. Many of the issues which need to be discussed and analysed will be similar throughout the department.

Time spent on considering how to work together can be repaid many times over, both in terms of making best use of resources and of meeting the needs of pupils with special educational needs. Less time will be wasted in 'game-playing' and in defending professional barriers. Greater understanding of how colleagues work and relate to each other can increase effectiveness enormously.

Teambuilding, however, should not be seen as the only answer. Critchley and Casey (1986) warn that there does not have to be teamwork for organisations to be effective. They suggest that it is necessary for strategic decisions but as these only happen sometimes, there is no need to work or be trained to work as a team all the time. In fact they feel that teambuilders work towards open attitudes willy-nilly where it may not be of prime importance. In some circumstances it is more efficient to get on alone, particularly when the 'level of certainty' about the job is high. There really needs to be balance between getting on with your own work and a degree of sharing. This collaboration is particularly needed when the 'level of uncertainty' in the work is high and more than one set of ideas will help to move things forward.

Despite this warning, we feel that training people together can only be beneficial. The more individuals know about each other, the better they can adjust to working together effectively. If there is going to be training in special education across disciplines and specialisms, then those holding the power and resources must be convinced that the time and money are worth spending. We are convinced of its importance and hope that the arguments put forward have convinced you.

Action research

Teambuilding taken from an industrial setting is not the only useful method upon which we can call whilst training teams of people to work collaboratively. Action research, which was developed in education through Stenhouse's Humanities Project in the 1960s, has much to offer.

> Action research is a form of self-reflective enquiry undertaken by participants ... in social (including educational) situations in order to improve the rationality and justice of (a) their own social or educational practices, (b) their understanding of these practices, and (c) the situations (and institutions) in which these practices are carried out.
>
> (Carr and Kemmis, 1986)

One of the most important points about action research is the fact that teachers are encouraged to become researchers in their own classrooms. They are encouraged to collect data from their own situations and use that to move their own practice forward. There is a spiral of enquiry which enables teacher-researchers to:

- identify problems or concerns;
- collect data;
- plan for action;
- implement the plan;
- evaluate;

and begin again. In one sense action research is never completed, there is always something else to be improved. However, in practice, projects often do have a beginning and an end.

The role of the facilitator is central to most action research, although teachers have been known to carry out this kind of research without the 'critical friend' to help them to problem-solve effectively. O'Hanlon (1991) describes the role of the facilitator as a combination of:

- enhancing professional development;
- exposing colleagues to a range of concepts, theories and models of knowledge to help them solve their problems;
- developing professional research skills;
- establishing professional renewal;
- enabling professionals to evaluate and respond to issues encountered in practice;
- enabling professionals to become more effective members of the educational community.

(O'Hanlon, 1991, p.74)

Somekh (1989) suggests that the role of facilitator is not a fixed one and could be a consultant working with teachers in the classroom, another teacher on secondment, the INSET co-ordinator, a senior teacher or as O'Hanlon, a lecturer in higher education. There is no reason why, when professionals are working together collaboratively, that they cannot act as facilitators for each other, although an outside pair of eyes is extremely useful. Holly (1984) points out that working together can be an important part of the process. 'Action research fosters collegiality, informality, openness and collaboration, across boundaries' (Holly, 1984). It sounds just the training method needed for working together across disciplines and specialisms.

Example
A teacher and an occupational therapist were attending the course for staff working with people with profound and multiple learning disabilities. They identified a problem with the timetabling and distribution of equipment. Much time was being wasted and pupils' individual programmes were not being completed. As this was a situation that affected them both, they decided to begin by collecting data which more accurately defined the problems. All staff in the unit were involved in this. From that they devised a written rota for equipment which was posted on the wall for all staff to follow. The evaluation and subsequent collection of comparative data

demonstrated some improvement but pupil programmes were still not being completed. In the next stage grouping of pupils was reconsidered so that staff could work more efficiently and waste less time moving between them. The cycle went on with new ideas at every step to improve the teaching and learning in the classroom.

The project had to come to an official end to fulfil the demands for assessment as part of the course, but the process did not stop there and the incidental learning that had happened as part of the project was enormous. The two members of staff got to know each other very well and began to understand more of the way in which they each worked.

An eclectic approach to training

Eclecticism has been suggested before in this book, and where training is concerned this seems potentially productive. If trainers or consultants can work directly with the groups or teams of people who work together regularly, then teambuilding techniques (including some of the theory about working collaboratively) can be extremely useful. Combining these with an action research project within their normal work day seems to provide a very powerful set of tools. The problems associated with 'hero-innovators' can be avoided and unlike most INSET, there will be a definite change in the teaching and learning in the classroom.

On courses where teams are not present all together, it will be necessary to rely on awareness techniques rather than try to develop specific skills, so that at the very least, individuals know of the problems and possibilities of working together and perhaps can persuade headteachers and managers of the importance of full team training.

It is said that 'there is more than one way of skinning a cat' and there are certainly many methods and techniques referred to in this chapter concerning training for collaboration. One thing that is immutable is the need for *something* to happen. Children with special educational needs deserve well trained staff, working together with the same aims in mind. Specific courses and workshops about how to achieve this are very important aspects of this training.

Part IV

The Way Forward

CHAPTER 8

Developing an Action Plan

In this final chapter, it seems appropriate to be looking forward positively whilst acknowledging the need for realism in a climate characterised by economic stringency. We are not going to make wild recommendations which involve spending thousands of pounds, but any change to the system is bound to have some cost or at least a redirection of resources. As this is a practical guide, we have set these recommendations within a framework of an 'action plan' to encourage a feeling that 'something can be done' to move practice forward and that there are alternatives to these kinds of comments:

> 'We do try to work as a team, but there is never enough time to meet.'
> 'My workload is too big to be in everyone's team.'
> 'Mrs A. doesn't understand what we're trying to do.'
> 'Meetings are just a waste of time.'
> 'If I spend time talking to you, there won't be time for me to do my real work, with Johnny and Mary.'
> 'We've tried teamwork and it doesn't work.'

It is very easy to be daunted by the difficulties that face individuals trying to change practice and end up doing nothing to improve the situation (see Chapter 7).

Action research

In order to understand the relevance of developing an 'action plan' for future collaborative work in particular situations, it is necessary to begin with an understanding of the approach from which it comes. Action research was introduced briefly in the previous chapter as a useful method for training professionals to work together. We would like to apply it at this point to encourage readers to examine their own institution or service and form their own plans of action to move practice forward. Development is never finished, and improvements can always be made.

Action research is sometimes characterised by a spiral or a series of cycles as professionals go through the following stages:

- identify a problem or focus for investigation;
- collect data related to this;
- conceive of a solution;
- devise a plan for action based on the conceived solution;
- carry out the action plan;
- collect data related to the action;
- evaluate what happened;
- reflect upon that in terms of the original focus.

At this point the cycle can begin again with a revised version of the problem or a related focus. It is a very powerful way of conducting research in work situations by the individuals who are directly involved. Being the subject of research by an outsider can be extremely revealing to those inside but the results can be more easily ignored than if the insiders conduct the investigation themselves.

Many practitioners feel that they have not been trained to carry out research and are consequently diffident about launching into what seems to be unknown territory. Hopkins (1985), amongst others, writes very convincingly of procedures which are already within the repertoire of most professionals. The whole idea of research is demystified and discussed in terms of observation, asking pertinent questions, trying out ideas, writing diaries, examining records and scrutinising videos; in short, doing all the things professionals do anyway. The difference is in that the approach is deliberate and organised. Data collection and evaluation are specifically employed and timetabled to enable the practitioner-researcher to be systematic in reflecting upon his or her work situation.

What must be emphasised at this point, is the necessity for the collection of data to be rigorous. It is easy for practitioners to be impressionistic and subjective in their view of their own situation (Webb, 1990). Pollard and Tann (1987) suggest four characteristics of good data collection, that it is:

descriptive (rather than judgemental)
dispassionate (and not based on suspicions and prejudice)

discerning (so they are forward-looking)
diagnostic (so that they lead us to better action)

(Pollard and Tann, 1987, p.27)

It can be difficult and time-consuming to collect worthwhile data, but it is always time well spent. Often potential solutions can reveal themselves during this procedure.

Example
A class teacher and a support teacher set out to try to increase the time available for discussing the needs of particular pupils. After studying each other's timetables, they agreed to make a note of any moment in the week when there was a gap, even if it was only ten minutes. The process of sharing workloads and commitment led to a simple solution, a regular quarter of an hour slot at the end of lessons on Thursday afternoons.

Making time to meet regularly actually began a whole new process of reflection which demonstrated the necessity for an examination of the complete support system, in terms of consultation between staff. More timetable examination and data collection concerning the use of support in class, led to a redistribution of time and priorities for everyone involved. The net result was a half-termly forward-planning meeting and a weekly exchange of information for record keeping purposes.

Systematic examination of the situation as it is at the moment, coupled with a desire for it to be changed means that in many cases, it is simple to alter the barrier to effective collaborative working at practitioner level. There are other times when the fieldworkers do not hold the power to enable fundamental change to take place. This is particularly so when funding across services is involved. Asking pertinent questions within the different services can, however, be the catalyst for those who do hold power to rethink what is happening. Directors of services are more likely to give due consideration to requests and suggestions if practitioners demonstrate a methodical approach to data collection and making a case for change.

Conducting an audit

The rest of this final chapter is designed to help practitioners to consider the different aspects of provision within schools and support services in a systematic and reflective manner. Questions to ask will be suggested which arise from the discussions which have formed the heart of this book. Areas for consideration within an audit will be highlighted so that an action plan can be devised which relates to specific teams or 'would-be teams'.

It has become fashionable to exhort professionals to carry out audits of their work (NCC, 1992; NCC, 1990; ILEA, 1982) and it is easy to feel overwhelmed by such procedures. Schools are already obliged to write School Development Plans and the procedure we are advocating can relate directly to this.

> The distinctive feature of a development plan (DP) is that it brings together in an overall plan, national and LEA policies and initiatives, the school's aims and values, its existing achievements and its needs for development. By co-ordinating aspects of planning which are otherwise quite separate, the school acquires a shared sense of direction and is able to control and manage the tasks of development and change.
>
> (Hargreaves *et al.*, 1989, p.4)

If priorities for collaborative work can be developed alongside other aspects of the work of schools and services, a set of realistic possibilities can be suggested.

If staff are going to feel in control of the audit process, they need to develop their own agendas and sets of questions to ask. This ensures that the process is relevant to individual situations. Thus we advise that our ideas are used as starting points but time should be spent devising an audit which directly relates to each situation. We emphasise that we do not envisage that all the questions we pose will be applicable for all the situations in which support teams can be found. Be selective!

Strategic level

It may seem strange to suggest that the audit begins at this level as, unless you are a director of education, social or health services, you hold no power or authority to make changes at this level. However, in the absence of a single service for meeting special needs, collaboration or at least inter-agency co-operation must begin here or fieldworkers will continue to be hampered by rules and conditions out of their control.

Suitable questions to ask in this area have been taken from various places as well as our experience, including Evans *et al.* (1989), Maychell and Bradley (1991) and Hunt (1979).

- What is being done to address the differences in structures, funding mechanisms and priorities within health, education and social services?
- What are the structures in place for LEAs, SSDs and DHAs to ensure effective implementation of new policies about common client groups?
- Who is responsible for inter-service co-operation?
- What joint planning and consultation is there between education, health and social services?
- How is financial responsibility for provision decided?
- How does each service know the extent of their role and how is role confusion and overlap avoided?
- How is information about individual pupils with SEN collected and collated? Does the structure encourage or actively facilitate collaboration?
- How are parents involved?
- How effective are the lines of communication between education, health and social services?
- Is there a policy statement or handbook setting out procedure for co-operation, available to all services?
- Does staff development include the chance for members of the different services to meet and discuss common strategies?
- When senior staff move on, what mechanisms are there to ensure that inter-service co-operation is continued?
- Is collaboration (or at least co-operation) in the job descriptions of key people?
- Is there an agreement about confidentiality and its extension across services?
- How often is inter-service co-operation reviewed and evaluated? Who and what is included in this review?

The ad hoc links that exist between education, health and social services will continue to frustrate real collaboration until such time as there is some form of regional or local initiative to support inter-agency work (Maychell and Bradley, 1991). In the absence of a single state department for services for people with special needs, the bulk of the work must be done at local and fieldwork level. One of the single most important factors is the appointment of professionals whose jobs include a significant amount of time for liaison between services. Initiatives will begin to happen if there are senior appointments made with this in mind. Directors of services must see it as a priority and must allocate resources or changes will not be made. Some of the stumbling blocks identified in Chapter 2 can be overcome if the will is there.

Operational level

This is the level at which heads of schools, support services and district officers decide how to manage priorities within their own section. An audit should include such questions as:

- What structure exists at head of service/school level to ensure effective collaboration?
- Whose job is it to liaise with other services?
- What is contained in contracts between services and in contracts between services and schools?
- How are manager's responsibilities defined where there is inter-service work?
- How are joint decisions made at managerial level?
- What joint training is available for service managers and for fieldworkers?
- What training is available for collaborative work/running meetings/interpersonal skills/team building?
- How are services organised to enable time for team members to meet for discussion?
- What has been done to enable team members to share physical proximity whilst they work in the field (sharing premises)?
- How are such potential problems as: status differentials/professional jealousies/service jargon/power games/conflicting loyalties handled as people work together?
- How are team members encouraged to work across the boundaries of their professional role ('role release')?
- How are team members chosen for each child's team? Is there any thought given to unnecessary overlap because of shared skills?
- How does the organisation of caseloads aid the timetables of fieldworkers?
- How is the keyworker or co-ordinator for each child's team decided?
- When do team members who service the same school get together to share information/skills/experience/knowledge?
- How are fieldworkers kept informed about decisions that affect them from any of the relevant services?

- What are the lines of communication between team members?
- In what way are parents involved in their child's team?
- What do job descriptions contain about collaboration?
- How are jargon-free reports encouraged?
- How often is inter-service collaboration reviewed? Who and what is included in this review?

This list was formulated from combining ideas from a variety of different sources, for example, Vaughan (1991); Gregory (1989); Losen and Losen (1985); Marshall *et al.* (1979) and Hunt (1979) as well as from our own experience.

As at strategic level, one of the most important factors in enabling collaborative work at operational level is the recognition of the need to allocate time for liaison. Contracts can help considerably here, by building in time for planning and evaluation. Support departments in mainstream schools would find it useful to draw up their own forms of contract with individual departments and teachers. This would be an excellent forum for the discussion of the vexed problem of where to find time to meet and plan.

Fieldwork level

The audit at this level centres round the way in which a support team achieves the overall aim of providing access to the curriculum for individual pupils. It focuses on the team itself and the way in which individual members contribute to making it effective. The work of Thomas (1991; 1992), Fish (1985), Steel (1991), Hunt (1979), Marshall *et al.* (1979), Losen and Losen (1985) and Rainforth *et al.* (1992) have been added to our own to compile the following list of questions to ask in order to build a picture of present practice. The questions are deliberately formed to encourage forward thinking as far as possible. There are a lot of questions but there does not have to be a response to them all. *They are suggestions.*

- Who is included in the support team/s?
- From which services do they originate? How does this affect their time/commitment/resources?
- What is contained in the school or service contract on collaborative teamwork?
- How often are full team meetings held? What influenced this?
- What arrangements are there for joint planning and regular exchange of information/assessment/records?

- How is it decided what kind support is being used: advising/direct support/in class support/withdrawal?
- In what way are parents part of the child's team? How are they encouraged to be effective members?
- How are individual programmes for pupils written? How do team members agree priorities? What evidence is collected to inform those decisions? How is the procedure evaluated?
- What is the procedure for ensuring that pupil priorities/general information etc. are communicated to all relevant staff?
- How does staff development include *all* staff? Is there joint training/exchange of skills and knowledge/joint problem solving/training for effective teamwork?
- What is the procedure for passing on information and inducting a new person when a team member moves on?
- How is professional jargon avoided?
- How are roles defined to avoid the potential conflict caused by two adults working in the same room?
- How do team members know what tasks they are to perform? Is everyone clear about team and classroom tasks?
- What steps are taken to avoid unnecessary overlap, particularly in assessment and record keeping?
- How does each team member work with pupils? Is there a blurring of roles when appropriate so that pupils receive similar input?
- How far is this input integrated into the curriculum and natural settings?
- What steps have been taken to reduce potential difficulties caused by professionals working together who have different backgrounds/funding arrangements/conditions of service?
- In what ways do team members support each other?
- What procedure enables team goals and priorities to be set?
- How is each child's core team decided? How many people does this generally include? Is the size conducive to effective teamwork?
- What procedures are there for calling upon a wider network of support when necessary?
- Of how many different teams is each support staff a member? Is this the most efficient division?
- Where are support staff placed physically? Can the proximity of the core team be improved?
- How is it ensured that 'everyone pulls their weight' in the team

and that no one person is left to do all the work?
- Who is the co-ordinator of each child's team? Does this vary according to need? Is this person the child's keyworker in the classroom?
- How effective are team meetings? What procedures are there for evaluating agendas/chairpersonship/decisions made/action taken etc.?
- What is the review procedure − for a) the work of pupils, b) the work of the team?

At fieldwork level, staff must be committed to working together. They must genuinely believe that joint efforts offer a better service to the pupils with whom they work or teamwork will continue to be half-hearted. It is very difficult to persuade doubters that after the initial struggle to find time, joint work becomes a way of life rather than a burden. Really it is worth the effort!

Moving forward

Conducting an audit is the first stage in the process of moving practice forward. The data collected as part of the procedure should be rich in information about present practice and the constraints under which everyone works. Some of the questions have been weighted towards suggesting an ideal and developing towards all of these at once is not possible. It is necessary now to decide upon priorities. These will be different according to whether the team under scrutiny is at a strategic, operational or fieldworker level. Each team, at which ever level, will be at different stages of development, so the result of this section will be unique to each situation.

The three lists which follow contain suggestions for the areas in which schools and services may wish to decide upon priorities.

Strategic level

1. Funding and resources across services (including cross service funding).
2. Inter-service co-operation (including communication and joint decision making).
3. Structures and roles (including appointments and job descriptions).

4. Staff development across services (including opportunities for training in collaboration).
5. Policy documents (including handbooks of information).
6. Review and evaluation procedures.

Operational level

1. Funding and resources within the service/school.
2. Collaboration at service/school level (including communication and joint decision·making).
3. Structures and roles (including appointments and job descriptions).
4. Staff development (including joint training opportunities).
5. Contracts and policy documents.
6. Review and evaluation procedures.

Fieldworker level

1. Resources at school level (including problems with overlap).
2. Collaboration within support teams for each pupil (including organisational procedures and joint decision making).
3. Roles and tasks of team members (including an agreement on which areas are shared).
4. Staff development (including opportunities for exchange of skills and knowledge as well as teamwork training).
5. Assessment and record keeping (including procedures for collaboration).
6. Curriculum delivery (including planning and working together in the classroom).
7. Review and evaluation (of both pupil progress and the teamwork process).

Writing the action plan

After the process of audit and deciding upon the priorities for immediate development, it is necessary to commit this to paper in a manner which enables evaluation to be carried out easily. Action needs to be decided upon and a time scale needs to be set against which progress can be measured. Special educationalists are skilled at writing objectives for individual pupils. That skill can easily be translated to objectives for themselves and their schools or services.

Example

The audit may have revealed two people working together in the same classroom who have very different ideas about how support staff should be used. Although it may be impossible for them to agree on every point, one of the priorities for the next term must be that they are given time to exchange views and devise an effective way of working together. Often misunderstandings occur because individuals are not given time to discuss their own points of view with each other.

Alongside this discussion should be more general staff development which increases the understanding those two individuals have of the nature of support teaching and the benefits of working together in an agreed manner.

Objectives might be written thus:

a)   Staff development sessions for this term will address
     i)   innovative support teaching techniques
     ii) ways of working together
b)   A and B will be timetabled for liaison sessions once a week.
c)   Class teachers and their specific support staff will produce brief joint report on their work together for discussion at the end of term team meeting (contents to be agreed during a staff development session).

Although none of this guarantees that A and B will work together more effectively, positive steps towards this goal have been taken and the discussion at the end of term will reveal whether the situation has improved. If it has not then further steps can be taken, involving further training or even moving staff so more compatible individuals are working together.

Final words

In this book we have offered practical guidance for working collaboratively in schools with pupils who have a variety of special needs. We have concluded with the basic structure of conducting an audit and developing an action plan for moving practice forward. Schools and services will no doubt be able to create their own lists of suitable questions, but those which we have identified can act as an initial prompt. Specifics can be added or taken away according to need.

We have urged, throughout the book, that school and support

staff consider very carefully the way in which they work together. Arguments have been presented to persuade those who work in special education in mainstream and special schools to examine their own work and reflect upon ways in which it can be further developed. Teamwork has become very popular over the last few years. Most of it is not very effective (Thomas, 1992) and much needs to be done in order to fulfil the exhortations contained within the pages of this volume. We recommend that you use the examples we have cited and the enthusiasm we have tried to convey to inch forward in your own practice towards the ideal of everyone working collaboratively to meet the diverse needs of all pupils.

References

Adair, J. (1984) *The Skills of Leadership*, Aldershot: Gower Press

Ainscow, M. (1991) 'Effective schools for all: an alternative approach to special needs education' in Ainscow, M. (ed) *Effective Schools for All*, London: David Fulton Publishers

Ainscow, M. and Florek, A. (eds) (1989) *Special Educational Needs: Towards a Whole School Approach*, London: David Fulton Publishers

Ainscow, M. and Muncey, J. (1981) *Special Needs Action Programme*, Coventry: Coventry LEA

Ainscow, M. and Tweddle, D. (1979) *Preventing Classroom Failure*, London: Wiley

Ainscow, M. and Tweddle, D. (1988) *Encouraging Classroom Success*, London: David Fulton Publishers

Ashdown, R., Carpenter, B. and Bovair, K. (1991) *The Curriculum Challenge*, London: Falmer Press

Aubrey, C. (1990) *Consultancy in the United Kingdom, its Role and Contribution to Educational Change*, London: Falmer Press

Audit Commission and Her Majesty's Inspectorate (1992) *Getting in on the Act. Provision for Pupils with Special Educational Needs: The National Picture*, London: HMSO

Backhouse, J. (1987) 'Changing teaching method through INSET', *British Journal of In-Service Education*, 14, 1, 25−8

Bailey, T.J. (1981) 'The secondary remedial teacher's role redefined', *Remedial Education*, 16, 3, 132−6

Barker, D. (1980) *TA and Training*, Aldershot: Gower

Barrs, M., Ellis, S., Hester, H. and Thomas, A. (1988) *Primary Language Record*, London: ILEA/CLPE

Barrs, M., Ellis, S., Hester, H. and Thomas, A. (1990) *Patterns of Learning*, London: CLPE

Bennett, N. and Kell, J. (1989) *A Good Start? Four Year Olds in Infant Schools*, Oxford: Blackwell

Bines, H. (1988) 'Equality, community and individualism: the development and implementation of the whole school approach to special educational needs', in Barton, L. *The Politics of Special Educational needs*, London: Falmer Press

Blenkin, G. and Kelly, A. (1981) *The Primary Curriculum*, London: Harper and Row

Blenkin, G. and Kelly, A. (1992) *Assessment in Early Childhood Education*, London: Paul Chapman

Bluma, S., Shearer, M., Frohman, A. and Hilliard, J. (1976) *Portage Guide to Early Education*, Wisconsin: Portage Project

210

Booth, T., Potts, P. and Swann, W. (eds) (1987) *Preventing Difficulties in Learning*, Oxford: Basil Blackwell

Booth, T., Swann, W., Masterton, M. and Potts, P. (1992) *Policies for Diversity in Education*, Milton Keynes: OU Press

Bowers, T. (1984) 'Power and conflict: facts of life', in Bowers, T. *Management and the Special School*, London: Croom Helm

Bowers, T. (1989) *Managing Special Needs*, Milton Keynes: OU Press

Bowers, T. (1991a) *LMS and SEN Support Services – Resource and Activity Pack*, Cambridge: Perspective Press

Bowers, T. (ed) (1991b) *Schools, Services and Special Educational Needs – Management Issues in the Wake of LMS*, Cambridge: Perspective Press

Bowers, T. (1992) unpublished lecture at University of Birmingham

Brian, J. (1992) *Team Development Workshop*, unpublished paper: Ashorne Hill Management College

Broadfoot, P. (1987) *Introducing Profiling: A Practical Manual*, Basingstoke: MacMillan

Burgess, R. (1985) *Issues in Educational Research: Qualitative Methods*, London: Falmer Press

Bush, T., Glatter, R., Goodey, J. and Riches, C. (eds) (1980) *Approaches to School Management*, London: Harper Row

Byers, R. (1990) 'Topics: from myths to objectives', *British Journal of Special Education*, 17, 3, 109–12

Campbell, J. (1989) *Assessing the National Curriculum: From Practice to Policy*, Leamington Spa: Scholastic Publications

Campione, J. (1989) 'Assisted assessment: a taxonomy of strengths and weaknesses', *Journal of Learning Disabilities*, 22, 3, 151–65

Carr, W. and Kemmis, S. (1986) *Becoming Critical: Education, Knowledge and Action Research*, London: Falmer Press

CATS (Consortium for Assessment and Testing in Schools) (1991) *Pilot 1991: General Issues*, London: CATS

Clough, P. and Lindsay, G. (1991) *Integration and the Support Service, Changing Roles in Special Education*, Windsor: NFER-Nelson

Clunies-Ross, L. and Wimhurst, S. (1983) *The Right Balance: Provision for Slow Learners in Secondary Schools*, Windsor: NFER-Nelson

Cohen, L. and Manion, L. (1989) *Research Methods in Education*, London: Routledge

Conway, J. (1989) 'Local and regional variations in support', in Davies, J.D. and Davies, P. *A Teacher's Guide to Support Services*, Windsor: NFER-Nelson

Coventry LEA (1987) *Topic Work Tasks*, Coventry: Elm Bank Teachers' Centre

Coverdale Organisation (1985) *The Practice of Teamwork*, unpublished paper

Cox, C. and Boyson, R. (eds) (1975) *The Black Paper 1975* (The Black Papers), London: Dent

Critchley, B. and Casey, D. (1986) 'Team building', in Mumford, A. (ed) *Handbook of Management Development 2nd Ed*, Aldershot: Gower

David, R. and Smith, B. (1987) 'Preparing for collaborative working', *British Journal of Special Education*, 14, 1, 19–23

David, R. and Smith, B. (1991) 'Collaboration in initial training', in Upton, G. (ed) *Staff Training and Special Educational Needs*, London: David Fulton Publishers

Davie, R. (1993a) 'Interdisciplinary perspectives on assessment', Chapter 8 in: S. Wolfendale (Ed.) *Assessing Special Educational Needs*. London: Cassell.

Davie, R. (1993b) 'Implementing Warnock's multi-professional approach', in: G. Upton and J. Visser (Eds.) *Special Education in Britain after Warnock*. London: Fulton.

Davies, J.D. and Davies, P. (1988) 'Developing credibility as a support and advisory teacher', in *Support for Learning*, 3, 1

Davies, J. D. and Davies, P. (ed) (1989) *A Teacher's Guide to Support Services*, Windsor: NFER-Nelson

Dawkins, J. (1991) *Models of Mainstreaming for Visually Impaired Pupils: Studies of Current Practice with Guidelines for Service Development*, London: HMSO

Day, C., Whitaker, P. and Johnston, D. (1990) *Managing Primary Schools in the 1990s*, London: Paul Chapman

Dean, J. (1992) *Inspecting and Advising – A Handbook for Inspectors, Advisers and Advisory Teachers*, London: Routledge

Department of Education and Science (1967) *Children and their Primary School (The Plowden Report)*, London: HMSO

Department of Education and Science (1970) *The Education (Handicapped Children) Act*, London: HMSO

Department of Education and Science (1972) *Teacher Education and Training (The James Report)*, London: HMSO

Department of Education and Science (1977) *Curriculum 11–16 (HMI Red Book One)*, London: HMSO

Department of Education and Science (1978) *Special Educational Needs – Report of the Committee of Enquiry into the Education of Handicapped Children and Young People (The Warnock Report)*, London: HMSO

Department of Education and Science (1978a) *Primary Education in England*, London: HMSO

Department of Education and Science (1981) *Education Act 1981*, London: HMSO

Department of Education and Science (1987) *National Curriculum Task Group on Assessment and Testing*, London: DES

Department of Education and Science (1987a) Press Release 343/87 'The Education Reform Bill' 20th November

Department of Education and Science (1988) *The Education Reform Act*, London: HMSO

Department of Education and Science and the Welsh Office (1990) *Discipline in Schools*, Report of the Committee of Enquiry chaired by Lord Elton, London: HMSO

Department of Education and Science (1989a) *Assessments and Statements of Special Educational Needs: Procedures within the Education, Health and Social Services, Circular 22/89*, London: HMSO

Department of Education and Science (1989b) *Standards in Education 1987–88*, London: DES

Department of Education and Science (1989c) *Records of Achievement (The RANSC Report)*, London: HMSO

Department of Education and Science (1990a) *Standards in Education 1988–89*, London: DES

Department of Education and Science (1990b) *The Education Order* (Draft proposals for assessment arrangements in English, Mathematics and Science), London: DES

Department of Education and Science (1991a) *Local Management of Schools, Further Guidance*, Circular 7/91, London: HMSO

Department of Education and Science (1991b) *The Parents Charter: You and your Child's Education*, London: DES

Department of Education and Science (1992) *Curriculum Organisation and Classroom Practice in Primary School* (The Alexander Report), London: DES

Department of Health and Social Services (1976) *The Court Report*, London: HMSO

Department of Health and Social Services (1986) *Disabled Persons Act*, London: HMSO

Department of Health (1989a) *An Introduction to the Children Act*, London: HMSO

Department of Health (1989b) *The Children Act 1989, Guidance and Regulations, Volume 6: Children with Disabilities*, London: HMSO

Department of Health (1990) *The Care of Children: Principles and Practice, Regulations and Guidance*, London: HMSO

Dessent, T. (1985) 'Supporting the mainstream: do we know how?' *Education and Child Psychology*, 2, 3

Dessent, T. (1988) *Making the Ordinary School Special*, London: Falmer Press

Dyer, W. (1977) *Team Building: Issues and Alternatives*, London: Addison Wesley

Dyson, A. (1990) 'Effective learning consultancy: a future role for special needs co-ordinators', *Support for Learning*, 5, 116–27.

Easen, P. (1985) *Making School-centred INSET Work*, Buckinghamshire: OU Press

Emblem, B. and Conti-Ramsden, G. (1990) 'Towards level 1: reality or illusion? *British Journal of Special Education*, 17, 3, 88–90

Evans, J., Everard, B., Friend, J., Glaser, A., Norwich, B. and Welton, J. (1989) *Decision Making for Special Educational Needs*, Loughborough: Tecmedia Ltd

Everard, B. and Morris, G. (1990) *Effective School Management*, London: Paul Chapman

Fagg, S., Aherne, P., Skelton, S. and Thornber, A. (1990) *Entitlement for All in Practice*, London: David Fulton Publishers

Fathers, J. (1990) *SATs at Blythe School – Preliminary Report*, unpublished paper: Blythe School

Fish, J. (1985) *Special Education: The Way Ahead*, Milton Keynes: Open University Press

Forsyth, P. (1991) *How to Negotiate Successfully*, London: Sheldon Press

Freeman, A. and Gray, H. (1989) *Organizing Special Educational Needs – A Critical Approach*, London: Paul Chapman

Gardner, J., Murphy, M. and Crawford, N. (1983) *The Skills Analysis Model*, Kidderminster: BIMH

Garner, M., Petrie, I. and Pointon, D. (1990) 'Survey of LEA Support Services' for a Meeting in London Special Educational Needs National Advisory Council in Booth, T., Swann, W., Masterton, M. and Potts, P. (1992) *Policies for Diversity in Education*, Milton Keynes: OU Press

Garnett, J. (1988) 'Support teaching: taking a closer look', *British Journal of Special Education*, 15, 1 and reproduced in Ainscow, M. and Florek, A. (eds)(1989) *Special Educational Needs: Towards a Whole School Approach*, London: David Fulton Publishers (pp.89–99)

Gilmore, M., Bruce, N. and Hunt, M. (1974) *The Work of the Nursing Team in General Practice*, Council for the Education and Training of Health Visitors, London

Gipps, C., Cross, H. and Goldstein, H. (1987) *Warnock's Eighteen Per Cent: Children with Special Needs in Primary Schools*, London: Falmer Press

Gipps, C. (1990) *Assessment: A Teacher's Guide to the Issues*, London: Hodder and Stoughton

Goacher, B., Evans, J. Welton, J. and Wedell, K. (1988) *Policy and Provision for Special Educational Needs: Implementing the 1981 Education Act*, London: Cassell

Gordon, V. (1989) *Your Primary School: Your Policy for Special Educational Needs*, NARE

Gregory, E. (1989) 'Issues of multiprofessional co-operation', in Evans, R. (ed) *Special Educational Needs: Policy and Practice*, Oxford: Blackwell/NARE

Guirdham, M. (1990) *Interpersonal Skills at Work*, Hemel Hempstead: Prentice Hall

Handy, C. (1985) *Understanding Organisations*, Middlesex: Penguin

213

Hanko, G. (1989) 'Sharing expertise: developing the consultative role', in Evans, R. (ed) *Special Educational Needs: Policy and Practice*, Oxford: Blackwell/NARE (p.67)

Hargreaves, D., Hopkins, D., Leask, M., Connolly, J. and Robinson, P. (1989) *Planning for School Development*, London: HMSO

Harris, T.A. (1970) *I'm OK – You're OK*, London: Pan Books

Hart, S. (1986) 'Evaluating support teaching', in *Gnosis*, 9, 26–31

Hart, S. (1992) 'Collaborative classrooms' in Booth, T., Swann, W., Masterton, M. and Potts, P. *Curricula for Diversity in Education*, London: Routledge

Hastings, Chaudhry C., Bixby, P. and Chaudhry-Lawton, B. (1986) *Superteams: A Blueprint for Organisational Success*, London: Fontana

Haynes, M.E. (1987) *Make Every Minute Count – How to Manage Your Time Effectively*, London: Kogan Page

Hegarty, S. (1987) *Meeting Special Needs in Ordinary Schools: An Overview*, London: Cassell

Hegarty, S. and Pocklington, K. (1981) *Educating Pupils with Special Educational Needs in Ordinary Schools*, Windsor: NFER-Nelson

Her Majesty's Inspectorate (1989) *A Survey of Support Services for Special Educational Needs*, London: HMSO

Her Majesty's Inspectorate (1991) *Interdisciplinary Support for Young Children*, London: HMSO

Hersey, P. and Blanchard, K. (1982) *Management of Organisational Behaviour: Utilising Human Resources, Third Edition*, Englewood: Prentice-Hall International

Hockley, L. (1989) 'Sharing information concerning LEAs' organisation of educational support services and developing the role of the support teacher', in Evans, R. (ed) *Special Educational Needs: Policy and Practice*, Oxford: Blackwell/NARE

Hogg, C. (1990) Team Building Fact sheet Number 34, *Personal Management Journal*

Holly, P. (1984) 'Action research: A cautionary note?', in Holly, P. and Whitehead, D. (eds) *Action Research in Schools: Getting it into Perspective*, CARN Bulletin No. 6 Classroom Action Research Network

Home Office, Department of Health, Department of Education and Science, Welsh Office (1991) *Working Together Under the Children Act 1989*, London: HMSO

Hopkins, D. (1985) *A Teacher's Guide to Classroom Research*, Milton Keynes: OU Press

House of Commons Select Committee on Education, Science and Arts (1989) *Educational Provision for the Under Fives*, 1, London: HMSO

Hoyle, E. (1988) 'Leadership and mission', in Glatter, R., Preedy, M., Riches, C. and Masterton, M. (eds) *Understanding School Management*, Milton Keynes: OU Press

Hughes, M. (1985) *Theory and Practice in Educational Management*, London: Cassell

Hunt, M. (1979) 'Possibilities and problems of interdisciplinary teamwork', in Marshall, M., Preston-Short, M. and Wincott, E. (eds) *Teamwork, For and Against*, Birmingham: BASW

Hutchinson, D. (1974) 'A model for transdisciplinary staff development. A nationally organised collaborative project to provide comprehensive services to atypical infants and their families' (Technical Report No. 8). New York: United Cerebral Palsy Association cited in Sontag, E. (ed) *Educational Programming for the Severely and Profoundly Handicapped* (1977) USA: The Council for Exceptional Children

Inner London Education Authority (1982) *Keeping the Special School Under Review*, London: ILEA

Inner London Education Authority (1985) *Educational Opportunities for All? (The Fish Report)*, London: ILEA

Jones, S. (1992) *The Human Factor: Maximising team efficiency through collaborative leadership* London: Kogan Page

Kelly, M. (1991) 'The Role of learning support: a trefoil catalyst?', *Support for Learning*, 6, 4, 171–2

Kerry, T. (1982) *Effective Questioning*, London: Macmillan Educational

Kerry, T. and Eggleston, J. (1988) *Topic Work in the Primary School*, London: Routledge

Knight, R. and Bowers, T. (1985) 'Developing effective teams', in Bowers, T. (ed) *Management and the Special School*, London: Croom Helm

Lawn, M. and Woods, R. (1988) *Team Building with Industry in Initial Teacher Education*, Aldershot: Indtel

Lawson, H. (1992) *Practical Record Keeping in Special Schools*, London: David Fulton Publishers

Lincoln, C. (1991) 'An evaluation of SEN support services', unpublished thesis, University of Birmingham in Booth, T., Swann, W., Masterton, M. and Potts, P. (1992) *Policies for Diversity in Education*, Milton Keynes: OU Press

Lindsay, G. (ed) (1984) *Screening for Children with Special Needs*, London: Croom Helm

Lloyd-Smith M. and Sinclair-Taylor, A. (1988) 'Inservice training for designated teachers', in *Support for Learning*, 1, 4, Stafford: NARE

Losen, S. and Losen, J. (1985) *The Special Education Team*, Boston: Allyn and Bacon

Lunt, I. (1987) 'Special needs in the primary school', in Thomas, G. and Feiler, A. (eds) *Planning for Special Needs: A Whole-School Approach*, Oxford: Basil Blackwell

Lyons, G. and Stenning, R. (1986) *Managing Staff in Schools*, London: Hutchinson

MacConville, R. (1991) 'A support services response to the 1988 Act', in Bowers, T. *Schools, Services and Special Educational Needs — Management Issues in the Wake of LMS*, Cambridge: Perspective Press

Marshall, M., Preston-Shoot, M. and Wincott, E. (eds) (1979) *Teamwork, For and Against*, Birmingham: BASW

Maychell, K. and Bradley, J. (1991) *Preparing for Partnership: Multi-agency Support for Special Needs*, Slough: NFER

McBrien, J. and Foxen, T. (1981) *The EDY In-Service Course for Mental Handicap Practitioners*, Manchester: Manchester University Press

McConkey, R. (1981) 'Education without understanding', in *Special Education*, 2, 1–28 and 8, 3, 8–10

McLaughlin, C. (1989) 'Working face to face: aspects of interpersonal work', *Support for Learning*, 4, 2, 96–101

Mulligan, J. (1988) *The Personal Management Handbook — How to make the most of your potential*, London: Sphere Books

Muncey, J. and Ainscow, M. (1983) 'Launching SNAP in Coventry', in *Special Education: Forward Trends*, 10, 3

Murphy, P. (1988) 'TGAT: a conflict of purpose', in *Curriculum*, 9, 3, 152–8

Myers-Briggs, I. (1962) *The Myers Briggs Type Indicator*, California: Consulting Psychologists Press

National Curriculum Council (1989) *Curriculum Guidance 2: A Curriculum for All*, York: NCC

215

National Curriculum Council (1990) *Curriculum Guidance 3: The Whole Curriculum*, York: NCC

National Curriculum Council (1992) *The National Curriculum and Pupils with Severe Learning Difficulties*, London: NCC

O'Hanlon, C. (1991) 'The facilitator's role in action research for teachers of pupils with severe educational needs', in Upton, G. (ed) *Staff Training and Special Educational Needs*, London: David Fulton Publishers

Orelove, F.P. and Sobsey, D. (1991) *Educating Children with Multiple Disabilities – A Transdisciplinary Approach*, Maryland: Brookes

Pascall, D. (1992) 'In Pursuit of Excellence', a speech on primary education, Cambridge Primary Headteachers' Conference, University of Leicester, 24th September

Payne, M. (1982) *Working in Teams*, London: MacMillan

Pearson, H. (1988) 'The assessment of reading through observation', in *Reading*, 22, 3, 158–63

Pearson, L. (1990) 'What the pilot SATs taught us?', *British Journal of Special Education*, 17, 4, 130–2

Pearson, L. and Lindsay, G. (1987) *Special Needs in the Primary School: Identification and Intervention*, Windsor: NFER-Nelson

Perrott, E. (1982) *Effective Learning*, London: Longman

Pollard, A. and Tann, S. (1987) *Reflective Teaching in the Primary School*, London: Cassell

Rainforth, B., York, J. and MacDonald, C. (1992) *Collaborative Teams for Students with Severe Disabilities*, Baltimore: Paul Brookes

Rance, P. (1971) *Record Keeping in the Primary School*, London: Ward Lock Educational

Reeves, J. (1991) 'Supporting change within schools: the development of advisory services', in McLaughlin, C. and Rouse, M. (eds) *Supporting Schools*, London: David Fulton Publishers

Richmond, R.C. and Smith, C. (1990) 'Support for special needs: the class teacher's perspective', *Oxford Review of Education*, 16, 3, 295–310

Robinson, K. (1988) *A Handbook of Training Management*, London: Kogan Page

Robson, C., Sebba, J., Mittler, P. and Davies, G. (1988) *In-service Training and Special Educational Needs: Running Short School-focused Courses*, Manchester: Manchester University Press

Rose, R. (1991) 'A jigsaw approach to group work', *British Journal of Special Education*, 18, 2, 54–8

Rouse, M. and Balshaw, M. (1991) 'Collaborative INSET and special educational needs', in Upton, G. (ed) *Staff Training and Special Educational Needs*, London: Fulton

Rowntree, D. (1989) *The Manager's Book of Checklists – A Practical Guide to Improving Managerial Skills*, Aldershot: Gower

Royal National Institute for the Blind (1992) *Curriculum Materials used with Multi-handicapped Visually Impaired Children and Young People*, report from the working party (MHVI) London: RNIB

Russell, P. (1990) 'Introducing the Children Act', *British Journal of Special Education*, 17, 1, 35–7

Salmon, J. (1987) *Training for the Management of Special Educational Needs*, Bristol: NDCSMT

Schools Examination and Assessment Council (1990) *A Guide to Teacher Assessment*, London: Heinemann

Scottish Education Department (SED) (1978) *The Education of Pupils with Learning Difficulties in Primary and Secondary Schools in Scotland: a progress report by Her Majesty's Inspectorate*, Edinburgh: HMSO

Sebba, J. and Robson, C. (1988) 'The development of short, school-focussed INSET courses in special educational need', in *Research Papers in Education*, 2, 1, 3–30

Sheridan, M. (1975) *From Birth to Five Years – Children's Developmental Progress*, Windsor: NFER-Nelson

Somekh, B. (1989) Action research and collaborative school development', in McBride, R. (ed) *The In-Service Training of Teachers*, London: Falmer Press

Staff of Tye Green School (1991) Broad, balanced ... and relevant', *Special Children*, 44, 11–13

Steel, F. (1991) 'Working collaboratively within a multi-disciplinary framework', in Tilstone, C. *Teaching Pupils with Severe Learning Difficulties – Practical Approaches*, London: David Fulton Publishers

Strauss, G. (1962) 'Tactics of lateral relationships: the purchasing agent', *The Administrative Science Quarterly*, 7, Sept. 161–86

Tann, S. (1988) *Developing Topic Work in the Primary School*, London: Falmer Press

Thomas, G. (1989) 'The changing role of the educational psychologist', in Dwyfor Davies, J. and Davies, P. (eds) *A Teacher's Guide to Support Services*, Windsor: NFER-Nelson

Thomas, G. (1991) 'Classroom organisation to meet special needs', in Hinson, M. (ed) *Teachers and Special Educational Needs*, Second Edition

Thomas, G. (1992) *Effective Classroom Teamwork: Support or Intrusion?* London: Routledge

Thomas, G. and Jackson, B. (1989) 'The whole school approach to integration' in Ainscow, M. and Florek, A. (eds) *Special Educational Needs: Towards a Whole School Approach*, London: David Fulton Publishers

Tilstone, C. (1991) *Teaching Pupils with Severe Learning Difficulties – Practical Approaches*, London: David Fulton Publishers

Tomlinson, S. (1982) *A Sociology of Special Education*, London: Routledge and Kegan Paul

Trethowan, D. (1985) *Teamwork in Schools*, London: Education for Industrial Society

Tuckman, B.W. (1965) *Developmental Sequence in Small Groups*, Psychological Bulletin

Vaughan, P. (1991) 'Rules of engagement', *Health Services Management*, 87, 3, 126–8

Visser, J. (1986) 'Support: a description of the work of the SEN professional', *Support for Learning*, 1, 4, 6

Ware, J. (1990) 'The National Curriculum for pupils with severe learning difficulties', in Daniels, H. and Ware, J. *Special Educational Needs and the National Curriculum*, London: Institute of Education

Webb, R. (1990) 'The processes and purposes of practitioner research' in Webb, R. (ed) *Practitioner Research in the Primary School*, London: Falmer Press

Wedell, K. (1985) 'Future direction for research on children's special educational needs', *British Journal of Special Education*, 12, 1, 22–6.

Wedell, K. (1988) 'The National Curriculum and special educational needs', Lawton, D. and Clutty, C. *The National Curriculum*, London: Institute of Education

West-Burnham, J. (1987) 'Effective learning and the design of staff development activities', *Educational Change and Development*, 8, 2, 17–23

Weston, P. (1992) 'A Decade for Differentiation', *British Journal of Special Education*, 19, 1, 6–9

Whitaker, P. (1990) *The Development of Advisory Teachers*, Centre for Adviser and Inspector Development, Wakefield in Dean, J. (1992) *Inspecting and Advising − A handbook for inspectors, advisers and advisory teachers*, London: Routledge

Willey, M. (1989) 'LMS: a rising sense of alarm', *British Journal of Special Education*, 16, 4, 136−8

Wilson, M. (1989) 'Teacher development and colleague consultation: the case of the school based resource teacher', in Thomas, G. *Effective Classroom Teamwork, Support or Intrusion?*, London: Routledge

Wood, D. (1988) *How Children Think and Learn*, Oxford: Blackwell

Woodcock, M. (1979) *Team Development Manual*, New York: Halstead/Aldershot: Gower

Woodcock, M. and Francis, D. (1981) *Organisation Development Through Teambuilding and Planning: A Cost Effective Strategy*, Aldershot: Gower

Woods, P. (ed) (1980) *Pupil Strategies: Explorations in the Sociology of the School*, London: Croom Helm

Woods, P. (1986) *Inside Schools*, London: Routledge and Kegan Paul

Zander, A. (1982) *Making Groups Effective, San Francisco: Jossey-Bass*

Name Index

220

Subject Index